SOUL SISTERS, COME ON TO MY HOUSE

*Discussing Cultural Sensitivity
and Human Kindness*

SUSAN FREIRE-KORN
AND HER SOUL SISTERS

iUniverse, Inc.
Bloomington

Soul Sisters, Come on to My House
Discussing Cultural Sensitivity and Human Kindness

iUniverse books may be ordered through booksellers or by contacting:

iUniverse
1663 Liberty Drive
Bloomington, IN 47403
www.iuniverse.com
1-800-Authors (1-800-288-4677)

Because of the dynamic nature of the Internet, any Web addresses or links contained in this book may have changed since publication and may no longer be valid. The views expressed in this work are solely those of the author and do not necessarily reflect the views of the publisher, and the publisher hereby disclaims any responsibility for them.

Any people depicted in stock imagery provided by Thinkstock are models, and such images are being used for illustrative purposes only.

Certain stock imagery © Thinkstock.

ISBN: 978-1-4620-1949-6 (sc)
ISBN: 978-1-4620-1951-9 (hc)
ISBN: 978-1-4620-1950-2 (ebk)

Library of Congress Control Number: 2011907330

Printed in the United States of America

iUniverse rev. date: 08/18/2011

The contents of this book, *Soul Sisters, Come on to My House*, reflects the author's views acquired through her experiences in knowing her soul sisters. This book represents the opinions and personal statements of the individuals and author who have elected to exercise their US constitutional rights to free, silent, and anonymous speech (i.e., the right to remain anonymous).

DEDICATION

"Rochelle"

The story I'm about to share with you is true. It is about human kindness at its highest level. It is about the littlest hero I know, who gave up her life to help others.

Rochelle was ten years old in the fall of 1992, when this tragic accident occurred. She lived in a wooden shack in the Russian River hills of California. I remember the Christmas before, she had asked for a "blanket and pillow of her own" for her presents. I made sure she got it that year, for she was a child of little means with a huge heart.

One October night about ten thirty, while her mother and boyfriend were not home, a fire took place in her house. The fireman said it was caused by "papers being placed too close to the fireplace downstairs." No one knows for sure, but it is suspected that Rochelle noticed the house fire and ran upstairs to save her two younger sisters, aged eight and six at the time. After waking them up and hurrying them to safety through an upstairs door that led to the outside, she hurried back downstairs to save the other two little girls (who were her mother's boyfriend's), ages five and three. However, by the time she reached them, the house was totally engulfed in flames, and all three girls perished.

When we as family members received the call the next day that the firemen could not locate Rochelle and the two other little girls, we knew the unreal had happened. So, what is the moral of this story? Here is a child just ten years old who had the mind-set to save her two sisters. Rochelle replaced fear with courage and went downstairs to try and save two other little girls. I believe this story speaks volumes about one brave, heroic little girl who understood at a very early age the act of human kindness. Rochelle is the littlest and bravest angel, with a hero's heart, who saved her two sisters before herself, and then left this earth with two other sisters. This is one tragic story with a big lesson in human kindness and love. May you rest in peace, our littlest angel.

CONTENTS

CONTENTS

PREFACE

This book covers the generational gaps between my soul mother, who is age ninety, to a few soul sisters in their forties—and some of us who are senior soul sisters, in our sixties. We have much to say about our lives and what has shaped us into the people we are today. These unique women address how they were raised and how they were able to "break the cycles" they did not want to bring into their present lives.

Sometimes people come into our lives for a reason or a season, and yet we may never know why. Then there are those people who come into our lives and stay a lifetime. I have chosen the soul sisters featured in *Soul Sisters, Come on to My House* to be with me for a lifetime. These soul sisters are unique, extraordinary women who have been through the trials and challenges of life experiences. They have been able to turn around whatever life handed them and make a different life for themselves.

Their new lives are full of human kindness and love. Through their life experiences, they have been blessed to become the masters of their own destiny. By sharing their life experiences, we hope that you too will discover what it takes to change a mind-set about treating everyone with dignity and respect. We *can* change the world to be a better place for all. I prefer to call it simply treating others with human kindness.

I could not have written a book about soul without mentioning the significance of religion and spirituality and how they play a major role in many of our lives. Human kindness must come from a place within our soul and our human spirit. The common theme here is to treat others the way you want to be treated. Throughout the book, there will be mention of religion or prayer as it relates to our everyday lives. It is in no way intended to influence or persuade one's thoughts or beliefs; it is to be used for informational purposes only. I will also share my own spiritual experiences when visiting churches and cathedrals in southern France, and how religion plays a vital role in my life today.

Recently, I had been praying about finding an answer and direction to writing my book, *Soul Sisters, Come on to My House*, because I felt I was missing a significant element in the content and theory of the book. I had been struggling with the challenge of how I was going to integrate spirituality and religion into a book that would be useful in diversity programs in employment organizations to help others understand cultural sensitivity and how to treat each other with respect, dignity, and human kindness.

In May 2010, I was returning to the beautiful site of St. Marie Magdalene Church. It was something I had dreamed about since my last visit to France. It is located in a little country town in the southern part of France, and it is not what I would consider a tourist place; the times I have visited, there were very few people, if any, in the church or grounds.

After viewing the beauty of this church, I went straight up to the altar area. It was as if I was drawn there, and something happened to me. While standing there, a bright, warm feeling entered my heart; it was as if it reached deep into my soul. If I could put into words what I felt, it would have said to me, "It is about human kindness and how we should treat others." I was spellbound and then instantly realized my book was about all that is good in the world. My book was about how we should treat each other with kindness, love, mercy, and compassion. *Wow!* I had experienced a vision in me that led me to the truth of my book. After I returned back to our friends, I realized the book was much bigger than cultural diversity for employment; it was about human kindness at its highest level. I had my answer.

Throughout the life stories of these women, some of the same questions will be raised and be answered, such as, "What does soul mean to you?" and "What does soul sister mean to you?" I believe doing so helps us to understand and not to judge others who may be different from ourselves.

Although this book is written by three African American women, three Caucasian women, and three Latina women, you will discover the similarities we all share as humans; we really are not all that different from each other. There is no difference when it comes to being a parent, a coworker, and a human being. It is these similarities we must hold onto to change a mind-set through understanding and educating ourselves about other cultures. We can do this by suspending judgment and not jumping to conclusions. Instead of going straight to conclusion and closing ourselves off, we need to learn more about others and how they can enrich our lives. Learning to listen to understand and learning to listen with compassion will help us as humans to identify with each other. When you shed yourself of all the old tales and beliefs you held as a child or from a bad experience, you can then open your heart and your mind to see the beauty there is in discovering and understanding others. It can open a whole new, fulfilling world for you.

We have all heard about heart and soul. Well, this is what this book's message is about—using your heart and soul to make it a better world for all.

I wish you strength in your journey to enlighten your thoughts with an open mind and make a difference in the world by opening communications with someone who may be different than yourself.

ACKNOWLEDGMENTS

I've been fortunate because God sent me some angels along the way. They are my soul sisters. This book could not have been written without the help, assistance, support, and approval of my soul sisters:

Linda Lake
Arrenia Corbin
Jean Jones
Lorna Holmes-Jacobson
Donell Allen
Miranda Sanz
Stephanie Rivera
Kathleen Freire-Valdez
Claire Newman

Thank you all for allowing me to share your life experiences, hopes, and dreams.

INTRODUCTION

It was a cold February, Presidents' Weekend 2008, in the Sierra Nevada foothills, and the snow had not yet melted on the frozen ground when I invited several women to come to my house and hear about my plan to write a book that would include them. To my surprise, all of them showed up except for one who lived in Portland, Oregon; she could not make it but was very interested in what I had to say.

As each woman came into my house, they all sat around my dining room table, eager to hear the news. I had plans to write a book about cultural sensitivity and taking people from the state of cultural awareness to cultural sensitivity. I had been retired from work about two years, but prior to my retirement, I had been working at a corporate level with cultural diversity in my service area and in the regional offices. I knew that most organizations were struggling with the transition from cultural awareness to cultural sensitivity. The main goal was to have employees treat each other with dignity and respect in the workplace.

My reason to have the women "come on to my house" was to inform them of my plan to write a book about cultural sensitivity. But most importantly, I wanted to use their life stories to help accomplish this task. I had thought long and hard about who would be the perfect women to have participate in making this dream a reality. My intention was to change a mind-set from feelings of indifference to opportunities to get to know others through understanding, acceptance, and kindness. If I could accomplish this goal within the workforce, this would be my great reward.

How did I select these very important women to be my soul sisters? I started off with who had made an impact in my life, who had contributed to my life, and who I had a drive or desire to learn more about. To my surprise, each woman agreed to the book project. They seemed eager and willing to contribute by sharing their life stories with me.

Over the next two years, we went to each other's houses and held meetings on how to go about writing their life stories. During these times, what happened for me was more than I could have ever imagined. The book evolved into more than I had ever thought it could become because from the process of writing the book, I learned understanding and listening with compassion; I got to know these women on a much deeper level. Going through the process brought me so much, which in turn became another gift.

I came to understand that the purpose of the book was much more than having a book written for the workplace to help others treat each other with respect, even though it did become that—and more. For me, the book *Soul Sisters, Come on to My House* is also a book about human kindness and spirituality. It was through the writing process that I discovered the real meaning of writing *Soul Sisters, Come on to My House.*

Each one of my soul sisters went through some very tough times and often spent years in despair and hardship. Yet they were able to lift themselves up through all the adversity to become very special and successful women in their own right. The best part is they did not let the hardships destroy them or keep them down. They were able to surpass any hardship and become their own person. As you read each life story, you will see that the individuals who entered their lives and caused such pain to them were not able to damage their spirit. Today, at work or in their personal lives, they have learned the values and rewards of treating all with respect and dignity.

I hope you will discover as you read this book the real meaning of life and how to apply it to your everyday life. It is about treating others not only with dignity and respect, but listening to understand, learning compassion, and sharing human kindness. It can also be about forgiveness and how we find the forgiveness when others treat us bad or hurt us.

It is my hope this book will diminish the mystery of fearing others who are different than ourselves. Life has many new starts and new beginnings. I know in my heart and my head that this book will serve a greater purpose and goal about how we should treat each other every day, and that is with compassionate listening and human kindness.

Understanding Cultural Diversity

THIS CHAPTER IS TO BE educational and informational only. It is in no way meant to imply, generalize, or stereotype any ethnic group. As you read my soul sisters' life stories, it will help you to understand cultural diversity, cultural awareness, and the cultural sensitivity that we are all unique individuals. The true, real-life stories of my soul sisters, who are of three different ethnic and cultural backgrounds, will help you to understand how all of this comes into play in our everyday lives of meeting and working with others who may hold beliefs and values different from our own.

For many years, one of my passions has been cultural diversity. I have been fortunate to expand on this interest because I was able to work closely on cultural diversity initiatives at my workplace as an educational instructor and facilitator.

Having this experience led me to realize there is still much to improve on regarding how we relate to each other in the workplace. Another aspect of my employment was to be a change agent and project manager in team leading and leadership development. When there were multiple issues in a department between employees, "peeling back" the onion revealed that many of the issues related to a lack of understanding and learning about other cultures. Much of what I learned and discovered led me to want to develop an effective way to manage diverse human relationships within our employee workforce. Through this process, it was my goal to improve cultural diversity by educating others about using compassionate listening and understanding skills to create a better performance in the workforce. Most importantly I wanted to see them use listening and understanding to affect how employees interact with each other.

After years of volunteerism, educational training, and facilitations, I was honored and humbled by receiving the R. J. Erickson Achievement Group Awards for years 2004 and 2005 from the Kaiser Permanente National Diversity

Program. The R. J. Erickson Diversity Achievement Award acknowledges those employees and physicians who have distinguished themselves through diversity advocacy, innovation, and service.

Cultural knowledge consists of learning and understanding characteristics of different ethnic groups' history, values, and beliefs. It also identifies the similar behaviors of cultural environments that cross over through all ethnic environments, such as individuals with disabilities, older adults, mental illness, health diseases, alcoholism, drug use, criminal activity, domestic violence, and suicide.

My soul sisters are African American, Latina, and Caucasian, but they share similar behaviors in their life stories of family histories, beliefs, and values. These beliefs and values may be similar or different from your own values and beliefs based on different life experiences and upbringings.

Cultural awareness is creating a learning and open environment for understanding and developing sensitivity of another ethnic group. It is also about allowing yourself to be open to others' thoughts and attitudes, which may differ from your own. One form of human kindness is exercising and practicing compassionate listening and compassionate understanding skills when communicating with others who are different from us.

In my soul sisters' stories, they will express their own painful experiences when others in their own family or outside factors, such as the general public, employees, or employers, did not treat them with cultural sensitivity. The painful reality of how we mistreat and abuse each other is vividly expressed in each story.

Cultural sensitivity is the knowledge and understanding that there are cultural differences as well as similarities that exist in all of us. It is my goal that we as Americans will treat everyone with dignity and respect. It is only through this process that we can ever hope to move forward into trusting each other.

I have discovered that when you have an open heart with a compassionate understanding, getting to know others who differ from us can lead to some pretty wonderful things that you would otherwise miss out on in life. If I had not put my first foot forward to educate myself and to have an understanding of the bigger world around me, I would not have realized that it would also lead me to discovering inner peace.

The key here is not to judge others but to suspend judgment and withhold conclusions until you offer everyone you encounter an open and compassionate understanding of the differences and similarities in all of us. Every person is a mixture of cultures and experiences. Each person is a unique individual and is a representative of their own cultural beliefs and values. It is up to us to have an understanding and realization that we must respect these differences and just maybe learn what it takes to make the world a better place to live.

UNDERSTANDING AFRICAN AMERICAN FAMILIES

As I read my soul sisters' life experiences, I discovered some elements that were common themes and findings when researching the cultures, beliefs, and values of their African American heritage. *A Provider's Handbook on Culturally Competent Care: African American Population,* 2nd Edition, from the Kaiser Permanente National Diversity Council and the Kaiser Permanente National Diversity Department was helpful as a resource for my information.

My soul sisters—Arrenia, Jean, and Lorna—are all middle class as defined by US socioeconomic status. As in all ethnic groups, when the medial income increases, so do the educational statistics. Other findings state there is a higher proportion of African American women than men who are employed in professional or managerial jobs. All of these women are professionals who serve or have served in managerial or senior roles within their employment. They are college educated and have excellent working knowledge and job experiences within corporate America, specifically in the health care field.

On a personal level, they all express how important family members and extended family members are to them. Each of their ethnic communities has played a major role in raising them or influencing them about their own cultural values and beliefs. Soul sister Arrenia speaks about how her family extends a helping hand to help others not only in the African American culture but to all.

Strong religious beliefs are traditional among African American families and their communities. These religious beliefs are an everyday mainstay in the African American culture and community. Arrenia explains how religion played a major role in her childhood, family values, and who she is today.

Family and friends play an integral part in coming together to support each other in raising children and being an extended family unit. It is not uncommon that African American children are raised by their grandmothers and may or may not have their parents living with them. Jean tells the story of how her grandmother raised her, and then others of her family or extended family would take her in and be an integral part of her upbringing. As she became a woman and a mother, her grandmothers also helped to raise her daughter when she was struggling to get a college education and begin a career in the workforce.

The African American family unit openly accepts others who are not blood related to be included in the family circle, accepted as part of the family.

Often non-blood-related family members are given names such as uncle, aunt, brother, or sister.

Family reunions and family gatherings may differ among my African-American Soul Sisters; however, Arrenia, Jean, and Lorna each explain in their own words the value of family and the joy and fun that surround their family units at these times.

As in all cultures and ethnicities, health and illness play a major role in our everyday lives. Unfortunately, health and illness play roles in how we live, eat, and play in this world. Our cultural differences in food preparation and consumption, levels of health care, and religious beliefs each play an important role in the level of health status for each of us.

African Americans have high rates of hypertension, diabetes, renal disease, cardiovascular disease, cerebrovascular disease, and cancer compared to other ethnic groups. For African Americans, the highest percentages of cancer are breast, colon, rectal, lung, and prostate. One of the most common diseases among African Americans is sickle cell disease, even though it is also found in other ethnic groups.

Sickle cell disease is an inherited blood disorder that affects one in five hundred African Americans and one in one thousand Hispanic Americans. According to PubMed Health, sickle cell anemia is a disease passed down through families in which red blood cells form abnormal crescent shape. (Red blood cells are normally shaped like a disc.) Sickle cell anemia is inherited from both parents. Sickle cell disease is much more common in people from South and Central America, the Caribbean, and the Middle East. Almost all patients with sickle cell anemia have painful episodes (crises), which can last from hours to days. These crises can affect the bones of the back, the long bones, and the chest (Sickle cell anemia—PubMed Health; http://www.ncbi. nlm.nih.gov/pubmedhealth/PMH0001554/).

My soul sister Arrenia was directly impacted by sickle cell disease when her young grandson was diagnosed. Arrenia's mother has battled breast cancer twice in recent years.

UNDERSTANDING LATINO AMERICAN FAMILIES

Respect and dignity are highly valued among the Latino culture. It is important to this culture that everyone is treated with dignity and respect, and they expect others to do the same with them. There is also a strong presence of social hierarchy in the Latino culture.

My Latina sisters—Miranda, Stephanie, and Kathleen—express in their stories how respect and dignity play a vital role in who they are and how they have been treated sometimes very differently than what their own beliefs and values tell them.

In 2002 a national survey of Latinos by the Pew Hispanic Center stated that English is the primary language of 25 percent of Latinos, 28 percent are bilingual, and Spanish is dominant for 47 percent (2002 Henry J. Kaiser Family Foundation, Menlo Park, California and Pew Hispanic Center, Washington, D.C. Pew Hispanic Center National Survey of Latinos).

My Latina soul sisters Miranda, Stephanie, and Kathleen are bilingual, but English is my dominant language. Miranda, Stephanie, and Kathleen all spoke English and Spanish in their household growing up.

Based on Kaiser Permanente's *A Provider's Handbook on Culturally Competent Care,* once Latinos go beyond immigrant status, they are more likely to increase their education, incomes, occupational mobility, and fluency in English (Latino Population. Kaiser Permanente National Diversity Council). Miranda, Stephanie, Kathleen, and I are all pretty much removed from the immigrant status that our forefathers had. All of our grandparents or heritage links come from Puerto Rico, Mexico, and Ecuador.

All of us Latinas are educated with college degrees and have attained middle to higher status incomes. Through hard work and determination, our lifestyles are middle to middle-upper class levels.

The labor force participation among Latinos is high, and much of the work performed in housekeeping services, restaurants, and farm work is done by Latinos in America.

Stephanie, in her life story, clarifies the real-life, true story of being a farmworker at age six and her experiences regarding school and basic needs while growing up in this culture.

Latino cultural beliefs and values in regard to language word terms and dietary factors can and will differ. These factors are based on which Latin American country your ancestors or ethnic background stems from. Miranda clearly states in her story the Puerto Rican word term differences and preferences in cuisine and food preparation as being different from the preferences of someone who is Mexican.

There are significant differences across the major Latino groups in terms of alcohol consumption, with Cuban men and women tending to be light drinkers and Mexican American men and women the heaviest drinkers and Puerto Ricans falling between based on information provided by Kaiser Permanente's *A Provider's Handbook on Culturally Competent Care: Latino Population.* Kaiser Permanente (National Diversity Council).

All of my Latina soul sisters, as well as myself, express how alcohol has impacted our cultural environment and family lifestyles.

One belief for Latino cultures is that being healthy and pain free are an integral part of being able to do your daily duties and responsibilities, which include family and social roles. I must confess that this is very much my own view of being healthy and stable. If I'm pain free and healthy enough to continue all my daily activities of tending to my family, household, and community duties, then I consider myself well. If I'm unable to perform any of these functions, it impacts how I view my general health and happiness.

Major diseases for Latin Americans are diabetes, renal disease, gallbladder disease, cancer, and tuberculosis. In Kathleen's story, she expresses herself as a caretaker of her father and describes his struggle with stomach cancer and her husband's fight with alcoholism. My own father was an alcoholic, and at an early time in my life, he was hospitalized for tuberculosis. However, I was too young to understand the full impact these diseases had on the family unit.

Religion is very important in much of the Latino culture and family unit. Many of us believe in a higher power and have our own way of communicating with God, either in prayer or speaking to him directly. Stephanie mentions in her story the conversations and questions she asks God in her private moments. Many of us in the Latino culture, as in all cultures, believe our loved ones who are no longer with us on earth watch over us in our everyday lives and protect us.

UNDERSTANDING CAUCASIAN FAMILIES

Caucasians are defined as having origins in any of the original peoples of Europe, the Middle East, or North Africa. My Caucasian soul sisters are Lanette, Linda, and Donell. Although I have Norwegian and German from my maternal grandfather and was raised by an Irish and Welsh stepfather, I tend to relate more to the Latino side of my bloodline. Fortunate for my cousin Kathleen, she had the opportunity to grow up to live in two cultures, her birth mother being German and her father being Latino. Lanette, Linda, and I were raised in a predominantly white neighborhood, with a sprinkling of African American, Latino, and Asian neighbors. The one exception is Donell, who is Caucasian and was raised in a predominantly African American neighborhood and community. In Kathleen's, Linda's, Donell's, and my life stories, alcoholism, drug use, and domestic violence impacted much of our lives.

Alcoholism, domestic violence, mental illness, and even suicide can come into all cultures. As my Caucasian soul sisters explain, each of these elements directly impacted their lives and the ones they love. In Linda's life story, she tells how a family suicide impacts the whole family and what a helpless feeling it leaves on one's mind and soul. For myself, I realized that mental illness played a role in my sister's behavior as a young adult, and as she made health care decisions later in her life. I experienced mental illness with my father when he was diagnosis with Alzheimer's disease.

Health risks are high in Caucasian families for heart attacks, cancer, and strokes. These diseases have impacted all of my Caucasian soul sisters' families. Linda speaks about her mother's illness with cancer and their last days together. Kathleen speaks about her caretaker experience with both her parents and their final moments together. Kathleen's mother suffered a stroke and was disabled for many years. Donell's mother died from heart disease at a young age. All of my soul sisters' lives were impacted with health risks and diseases. My own experience with caring for my mother having breast cancer is very much a part of who I am today.

The common threads we all share as human beings are the importance of family and family gatherings, health and illness, religious beliefs, and how we all celebrate with food, drink, and play.

My soul sisters have bared their souls in the writing of their life stories. It will be evident how each of my soul sisters created her own survival skills and how each was determined to create a better life and to become the person she was meant to be. Whether you are white, brown, black, or polka dot, we all want the same in life—to be treated as equals and to be heard and understood. Practicing respect and dignity would make a better world for all of us. Once we have accomplished this feat, we can all move on to trusting each other.

I tell my own story through the stories of my soul sisters, how I met them and where I was in my life during the time I met each of them. I also explain why they were selected to be my soul sisters and why they are so special to me. I have not only learned to respect my soul sisters and treat them with the dignity they each deserve, but I can also say I trust them with my life.

INTRODUCING SUSAN FREIRE

I WAS THE THIRD GENERATION born of my family in San Francisco on September 16, 1946. I was an after-the-war baby and among the many who were later to be called the baby boomers. By the time I was one year old, my mother was already seeking a divorce from my Latino father. For the next few years, my mother, sister, and I lived alone in a small apartment on San Jose Avenue in San Francisco. There was no money or anyone to babysit us when my mother left for work as a chambermaid each morning. My sister was only three and a half years old and I was a baby of about one year old when we were left alone for hours until mother returned from her workday. My sister was so traumatized by my mother's absence that she spent most of the day crying and holding onto the doorknob until my mother returned. I was placed in the playpen, and my only saving grace was that I was too young to know what was going on.

By the time I was four years old, my mother had remarried, and we moved to Daly City, California. We lived on Bellevue Avenue in a diverse neighborhood. Mostly the neighborhood was predominantly poor white working class, but up the street there were more culturally diverse families, consisting of Filipinos, Latinos, and African Americans. Living in a diverse neighborhood really helped me as I grew up and entered the adult world. In our house, I was raised by my mother, who was Portuguese, Norwegian, and German, and my stepfather, who was Irish and Welsh.

In my adult years, I had a psychologist tell me my mother did love me but she had her limitations. The best I can say about this statement is that my mother was not raised by her biological mother. Her mother had died of breast cancer when my mother was four years old. Therefore, my mother was raised by her five older sisters and a stern father. I truly do not believe love and affection was expressed in the cultural environment in which my mother was raised. I believe this is the reason why I, as her child, was never exposed to a warm, loving environment from my mother. From the start, love and affection were absent from my life and my house on Bellevue Avenue.

Upon reflection, my thoughts as an adult are that by the time my mother met and fell in love with my father, who was Mexican and Ecuadorian, I think she was overdue for some passion in her life. My father, being Latino, had much love and affection to give to my mother. The only problem was that he had always enjoyed the company of other women and he abused alcohol. My mother once told me she went through the windshield of a car in which my father was driving drunk. I think she had enough of my father's alcoholism, even if he was charming when sober.

My stepfather was an alcoholic too. He was very different from my own father because he was extremely violent and physically and mentally abusive to me. The beatings started when I was six. My sister, who was older than I, also experienced the abuse until she was old enough to leave the home and get married at a young age. I will complete the rest of my story as I introduce my soul mother and soul sisters, who have helped me through trying times of my life. They are not only dear to my heart but part of my soul.

INTRODUCING SOUL MOTHER
CLAIRE NEWMAN

"THE OTHER NEWMAN"

LET'S BEGIN WITH SOME PEOPLE who were my first childhood neighbors that I never knew would be with me for a lifetime. Lanette Newman was my first best friend. As fate would have it, we lived next to each other in the old neighborhood of Daly City, California. Daly City is located seven miles from the heart of San Francisco and is, as they call it, "The Gateway to the Peninsula." Lanette's house was located on Oliver Street, and I lived on the cross street on Bellevue Avenue. Lanette's backyard spanned six house backyards on my block, and at the end it joined with my backyard.

No one knew the secrets that lived inside the walls of my house. It was a very dysfunctional environment, where fear and terror were more prevalent than kindness and love. The cultural norm at my house was to be seen and not heard. When dinnertime came, you were to eat without saying a word because no one was interested in what you had to say. At television time, if you got off the sofa and slid onto the floor of the green shag rug, you were sent to bed. Your thoughts, feelings, and needs were not of any interest in this house. Your sole purpose in our house was to meet the needs of your parents, whether that be keeping the house clean and the yard clean or whatever their requests were. There was no affection expressed, and no one ever said, "We are proud of you" or how good your report card was or any acknowledgment of your accomplishments when you received an award at school. No one showed any interest in what you were doing, and no one ever attended your school sports games, school celebrations, or important events.

You were fed and learned at an early age how to clean yourself. You were given a bed with covers and if you were lucky, a pair of shoes when yours had holes in the soles and you stuffed them with paper so your socks would not rip, or the shoe soles flapped and you then had to put a rubber band on them to keep from tripping on them; and maybe, just maybe, you would get two outfits when the school year started.

But fear was plentiful in my house. You were fearful of getting hit, you were fearful of what type of mood your mother or stepfather would be in based on their mental state, and you were fearful not to get in the way of their wrath when they were on a rampage, whether drunk or sober.

However, at my little friend Lanette's house, things were completely the opposite. My earliest memory of knowing Lanette is about age six; however, I'm sure I knew her when I was only five. One of the things that intrigued me at Lanette's house was she had a dollhouse that was adult size at the end of her yard. I believe it was painted white with green trim. As I peered from my backyard and gazed upon this perfect playhouse, I could not help noticing the dirt and weeds that accompanied me in my own backyard. In my yard, there was only a lonely, unpainted swing set my real father had built for my sister and me. The swing set was dear to me because my real dad made it for us with wood seats and strong chains to hold us. However, my stepfather failed to paint it, so rust formed on the bolts and hinges after a few years of wear and tear from the winter seasons. So there I sat on that swing set, just gazing at the playhouse that looked so perfect and wondering when I would be invited to come over and play in it. Time and time again, Lanette would hang out of her bedroom window, which faced my backyard, and yell out to me while I was in my yard, "Susie, can you come over to my house and play?"

I loved those welcoming invitations because it was always more fun to play at Lanette's house. Lanette was of average height and kind of chubby for a kid at age six, but she had a beautiful, welcoming smile. She had dark brown eyes, long brown hair, and an olive complexion. Lanette had a sister named Cheryl, who was one year older than she. Cheryl was fair-skinned, kind of tall, and slender. They had three younger brothers, who always seemed busy playing around the house with each other.

Lanette's dad, Dave, was busy at work most of the time because he held down three jobs. His main job was working at Lawry's Pavement Company weeknights, and weekends he worked as an usher at the Avenue Movie Theater. In addition, he was also a volunteer firemen for the Daly City community. So we kids rarely saw him, and when we did, he was usually grouchy and yelling about one thing or the other to get his point across. But as time went by, I realized his grouchy mannerism was probably caused by sleep deprivation. He was tall and had an olive complexion and dark hair and eyes just like Lanette's. He was both Mexican and Jewish but was baptized a Catholic on his mother's side.

Dave's better half was his wife, Claire Newman. She was truly the Harriet of the Ozzie Nelson family or the June Cleaver of *Leave it to Beaver*. She had long blonde hair, blue eyes, a fair complexion, and a beautiful figure in white shorts and halter tops, with long legs and wearing platform sandals in the summertime. She was very pretty and always had a smile on her face, even when she was busy cleaning and picking up after five children. She never missed fixing breakfast, lunch, or dinner for her children. If I was over there playing with Lanette, I was always included for mealtime.

As I look back many years later, Claire Newman is my "soul mother." She represents love, a safe place for me to go, and a warm, loving home environment; she helped me to understand family values. No wonder she is named after St. Clare, the patron saint of the poor. It was Claire who taught me at an early age the beliefs and values of learning acceptance, respect, dignity, and authenticity.

Yes, even if they did not know it, I was the "other Newman." Many times Claire did not have just five children; with me, she had six kids. Claire's heart was big enough to love all of us. I do not remember her ever scolding me or getting upset with me. All I have are memories of a kind, warm, beautiful woman who took on the role of loving mother for all her children, and that included me.

"HEART OF MY HEART"

Some of my best memories of the 1950s are of Claire playing the piano in the rumpus room downstairs. Lanette, Cheryl, and I would sing songs that were on the hit parade, songs like "Heart of My Heart." Another great song was "Lady of Spain," and Claire could play many favorite tunes of the day on her piano. It was a time of watching *Your Hit Parade on TV, The Mickey Mouse Club, Mighty Mouse cartoons,* and TV commercials about popular products of the day like Toni hair permanents, Halo shampoo, and Old Gold cigarettes. Pabst Blue Ribbon Beer commercials played during the Friday-night fights.

When summer came, I was often invited to join Lanette and her family to go to their aunt Mary's house in Marin County to go swimming in the pool. I remember the wind blowing through our hair with the top down in Claire's 1952 green Cadillac with tan leather upholstery while crossing the Golden Gate Bridge. When at Aunt Mary's house, all of us kids could not wait to jump in the pool. Then later we would all sit around the picnic table for lunch. Claire would go around the table with a half sandwich that was left over on the platter. She would offer it to each one of us to take just a bite. At lunch, we always had potato chips, sodas, and popsicles of any flavor.

Lanette and I spent many years together as best friends. We walked to school together all the way through our junior and high school years. We walked to church together for years. I cannot count the times I slept over at Lanette's house, sharing her bed with her. Claire always had a good-night kiss for me too when she tucked her children safely in their beds at night. I could not wait until my turn came for that good-night kiss. Little did Claire know hers would be the only kisses I ever got as a kid. My own mother thought those acts of kindness were just plain silly and not needed. It was through all these experiences that Lanette, her family, and I bonded for a lifetime.

When Lanette's dad thought I was spending too many nights over at their house, I would hide way down under Lanette's bedcovers when he came in to check on his kids at night. Since I was small in size, he never knew I was there. I stayed there until he went to his bedroom to retire for the night. By the next morning, he was already gone to work before we kids got up.

It was always better to spend time at Lanette's than at my own house. At Lanette's house, there was love and understanding of what it is like to be a kid and our growing-up stages. As I mentioned, my home was filled with strict rules of being seen but not heard and doing all the chores in silence. The unspoken rules were: "Do not speak your opinion because no one wants to hear it" and "If you're gonna cry, go to your room because no one wants to hear that either." Worse yet was, "If you cry, I'll give you something to cry for." By the time I was nine years old, the spankings turned into beatings with a thick leather belt by my stepfather. Mom loved to pull your hair and slap your face; when I reached my teen years, she began to beat me and tear off my clothes in anger. These were common occurrences at my house, and it was always a no-win situation. You could never do enough of your share of the work in the house and in the backyard. My mother and stepfather never let up on my sister and me. We were not safe in our own home. Our home was a place of danger, uncertainty, fear, shame, and terror.

No wonder I enjoyed going to Lanette's house, because the cultural environment was safe, warm, and loving, and filled with kindness. It was a huge relief from my crazy house of yelling, screaming, swearing, and drunkenness. The Newmans never knew about the abuse that went on in my house. Even when I became pregnant at sixteen and my life was unbearable at home, I could not bring myself to tell Claire or Lanette what was going on. When I left home at age sixteen, I wanted to run to the Newmans' house but was too ashamed to tell them how I was being beaten and verbally abused by my mother and stepfather and that I was now pregnant.

Yes, Lanette's house was a place where I could be safe. At Lanette's house, I learned what was normal in family values. I could also be myself and be authentic. If I wanted to act silly, it was okay and accepted. Throughout our childhood years of earthquakes, neighborhood fires, and everyday events,

Lanette and I became inseparable. One Halloween we dressed up like boys to go trick-or-treating. Another Halloween, we dressed up like bohemians, with white tunic dresses and long beads around our necks and straight, long hair and bangs.

When we went on to junior high school, we would many times walk the three miles from school to home. Often we would stop by the corner grocery store on Templeton Street. Lanette would buy a big bag of barbeque potato chips. In those days, a large bag of barbeque chips cost only a quarter. This was really a treat, and we would lick our red/orange fingertips all the way home.

All through our growing-up years, Claire was there to be a support to us. When the time came for us girls to start wearing bras, Claire was there to teach us how to put them on correctly so we would get a good fit. I remember standing in Lanette and Cheryl's bedroom as Claire showed us how to put our bras on correctly. Thank God for her because her guidance and love were never duplicated in my own home. At Lanette's house as a child, I was treated with respect and could always be myself.

At Lanette's house, her mom and dad's master bedroom was pretty much off-limits for the kids. I knew better than to go in there, so the only times I ever stepped in their bedroom were when Lanette and I were together. Usually the only time she entered was when she needed lunch money from her parents to go to school and her dad was still in bed. One time, though, I had the opportunity to see between the master bedroom and the main bathroom, which joined together with her parents' bedroom. My eyes saw something really beautiful—her mother's vanity dresser. To a young girl who had never seen a vanity before, this was something special. When I looked upon the small, white, wooden bureau and the mirror that accompanied it, I had a strange feeling. This was not a work area or a storage area, but a place for beauty and for you to beautify yourself. The little stool had a small padded seat cover, and it all looked so dainty and stylish.

I wondered how it would feel to sit there and look into the mirror; maybe your hair could be combed with kindness, instead of being pulled in a fit of anger. This to me was a place of beauty and relaxation. I was so moved by seeing the white vanity and mirror that I will never in my lifetime forget the wonderful feeling it represented to me at that time. It was a place just for Claire to sit and beautify herself. That vanity dresser brought a piece of magic to my life because now I knew there was more to home than just cleaning and doing chores.

By the time high school came along, I wanted to be more and more out of my house and spend more time at Lanette's house. At home my stepfather's drunken rages and abuse were becoming a daily event. If he fell asleep on the sofa after a drinking binge and someone or something woke him up and you were in his path, watch out. He would think nothing of picking you up by your hair, opening the front door, and throwing you down the concrete and marble staircase. His drunken behavior was out of control, and worse yet, my mother started to look the other way and have a blind eye to it.

In school Lanette and I had good grades. The time came when Lani (which was her nickname) became a pep girl and I became a cheerleader. These were the fun years when we discovered boys in a big way. Lani never really ever committed to a boy as a steady, but I had several boyfriends from junior high through high school. No one thrilled me more than Rick Lopez. He had plenty of free time and a car, and was known as a tough kid. It should have scared me, but instead I felt more protected in his presence. I had never felt love and affection from anyone and never from a boy. So I should not have been surprised when, about a year later, I got pregnant at the age of sixteen. I was disowned by my mother, and as far as home life, I was on my own. My pregnancy bought me a ticket out of the house and into the world of the unknown. I learned in time that the past as I knew it was over, and it was up to me to create my own future. I could only move forward because there was no looking back or going back.

Reflecting on my childhood days, I guess you could say Lani was not only my best friend but my first soul sister. Throughout my years of growing up, she would come in and out of my life. She was the godmother to my second son. I think she visited me at pretty much every place I lived during those turbulent times. Then as time would have it, we went our separate ways for many years.

We continued to send Christmas cards to each other and write a line or two, but I actually thought all those fun times we shared were over. I discovered many years later, when we were in our sixties, yes, sixty years old, that we lived relatively close to each other. Just a mere forty minutes away. My dear best friend and soul sister came back into my life. What a blessing for me. Now we see each other often and go over to each other's homes for dinner or just a visit. I have met her husband, Roger, who also lived in our old neighborhood in Daly City. Both our husbands get along really well, and therefore we see more of each other. Roger just completed building a beautiful swimming pool behind our home, and it looks perfect. Whenever I have a celebration or party, I'm sure to invite Lanette and Roger to share in more fun and laughter.

When I visited Lanette's home in Folsom, California, she was showing me her house, and in her master bedroom, I discovered a vanity and mirror just like her mother's. How it brought back so many childhood memories.

It was many years later that I would go to Lanette's childhood house to visit her wonderful loving mother, Claire. On November 16, 2009, I picked

Lani up at her home in Folsom. It was in the morning, and we were both excited to be out for the day to go see her mother in Daly City. Claire was eighty-nine years old, and I secretly wondered how many more opportunities I would have to see the sweetest, kindest woman I knew. Although the ride was more than two hours, time seemed to fly as Lani and I reminisced about the good old times we shared in our childhood. As we approached the old neighborhood, I realized how the streets seemed so narrow for the GMC truck I was driving; I had the feeling that not much had changed.

There was Claire at the top of her staircase, her hair now gray but all smiles, just like I always remembered her. She hugged us both, and quickly my heart began to race. She gave us a tour of the old house, which had a few updated rooms but I can still remember where Lani and Cheryl's bedroom was and where their twin beds were placed. Lani's bed was always near the window, where I could still see my old home on Bellevue Avenue. So many mixed emotions went through me as I peered once again through her window and found the house of my childhood.

Lani's brother's room had changed from a bedroom into a family room for Claire to watch TV with her doggy, Dolly. Claire's bedroom had not changed except for updated furniture; she still had her vanity. I looked at it with the same pleasure as I had so many years before—nothing seemed to change. Claire mentioned Dave, her husband, had made it for her. I thought to myself what an act of love it was for his beautiful bride.

The living room was beautiful and so well kept. I remember watching TV and seeing the old black-and-white movie of San Francisco with Lani and her mom one night at midnight when we were about twelve. Claire cried, and Lani said she always cries at movies; she even cried at the *Ugly Duckling*. But that was Claire's tender heart, always thinking about the one who was the misfortunate.

The dining room was just past the living room, and I remember the first time they got new rugs in there. Lani, Cheryl, and I think her brother David were playing with me and got around to tickling me so much that they refused my pleas of "I'm going to pee my pants." It was all a joke to them until here came the warm pee that streamed down my pants legs and onto the brand-new carpet! At that moment, all three looked shocked as I relieved myself. Funny, I never got in trouble that day, and there was no phone call to my parents to tell them what their unruly child did in the living room and worse yet, to their brand-new carpet.

Ah, but the kitchen is where I remember most my memories of sitting down at the little kitchen table while all the kids either ate breakfast, got their popsicles out of the refrigerator, or just plain spent time there talking and hanging out.

It was time to go have lunch, and Claire decided to drive her little white Oldsmobile to Westlake Joe's. At age eighty-nine, she was quick with "the pedal to the metal" as she whisked us around the old neighborhood and to the Westlake area. No problem finding a parking space, and she was out of the car before I could get my door open. I was amazed by her spunk and vigor. She had no problem getting around and was very quick on her feet. I was just amazed! She put a new meaning for me on being elderly, and I was delighted. I told Claire that of all the original people from our neighborhood, I'm glad she is the one still here with us.

Joe's in Westlake was an Italian restaurant and one that was dear to my heart as well. My dad and his wife Norma had spent many times eating there and were known as regulars. Westlake Joe's has the best raviolis and sauce, and I always order the fried prawns. As we looked at our menus, I told Claire and Lani this was where I went for my eighth-grade graduation dinner with my mother and stepfather. It was the first time I went there, and I felt everything was so fancy, with the waiters in tuxes. Claire and Lani followed my lead and ordered raviolis and prawns too. We all delighted in eating and enjoyed the good food and conversation.

Before I knew it, we were back at Claire's house. This time we went through the basement, and I could see all the old posters of movies of the past, just as I had remembered them. We went into the rumpus room, and there was the old piano of which I had such fond memories of Claire playing and us girls—Cheryl, Lani, and I—singing songs. Then Claire did something really special for me: she played the piano again for me. It was a song I did not recognize from the 1940s, a boogie-woogie, and she played like none of the years had passed. I loved it and knew this was a very special treat.

Once again in the kitchen, Claire set the table with a porcelain teapot of Royal Albert that I bought as a gift for her eighty-fifth birthday. There were cookies, tea, and vanilla ice cream as she took joy in serving us. I thought to myself, *Life does not get any better than this.* Seeing a wonderful old friend like Lanette and being able to sit once again at her mom's kitchen table.

I interviewed Claire for my book *Soul Sisters, Come on to My House.* She never hesitated as I asked her questions like "What is love?" and "What is happiness?" Claire remained true to her form when she talked about the importance of family and children, and how she had done everything for her husband because that was what she thought her role was. I remember because I was there. All the days and nights I stayed at Lanette's, all the many hours of playing over there, Claire never yelled at her children or had a harsh word for any of us. Yes, I was truly the other Newman at Lanette's. Claire never let me feel any different than that either. I learned so much from interviewing Claire, and I discovered what made her the loving woman she was in my childhood and the loving woman she continues to be today. One of the connections I had was when Claire said her parents were French and Italian and that they always showed kindness to others. When her parents prepared a meal for dinner, they always made a lot because you never knew who would be coming by during that time. Claire's parents' values and beliefs had rubbed off on her; that is exactly how I was treated whenever I went over to the Newmans.

Claire added, "My mother was a very giving person, so you got the feeling that when you cooked, you cooked a lot so if someone did come by, you had enough for all to eat. She always wanted to help people. My father was giving too, so we were brought up that way."

CULTURAL BELIEFS AND VALUES THAT NEVER CHANGE

Claire's foremost value is to be thankful that you are here every morning and not let anything depress you or get you down. "Try to be happy and do not hold a grudge against anybody, even if they do something to you and you do not like it." Another value Claire believes in is, "Try to always look your best and be the best you can be."

When we spoke about love, Claire said, "Love means something like you have to want to be with that person, do things for them, and respect whatever they do. Like Dave, my husband—I waited on him hand and foot, but I thought that was your duty, that's what a wife is supposed to do. Then, after a while, it is something you want to do, not something you have to do."

Happiness to Claire is to be thankful about everything you do and to be happy about it. "I'm happy just being healthy and getting up every morning and being able to do the things I want to do and having the time to do them."

Claire forgives easily and does not harbor ill feelings about anyone. She said, "I just do not let things bother me. It is just something that I forget about and let it go in one ear and out the other. Do not dwell on anything like that because if you dwell on anything, you are going to go nuts."

For Claire, being the wonderful mother she is, the most difficult thing for her is when her children get sick. She worries about them and wonders if they are going to be okay. "When Lanette was just a baby, she got pneumonia, and she was only two years old. We did not have a lot of penicillin then, and the doctor said to watch her during the night so that she didn't get uncovered. Well, I slept on the floor all night long for a week to watch her," said Claire. I asked, "What were your greatest fears?" She answered like the loving mother she is: "I think one of the times was when my daughter Cheryl had a brain aneurism. She did not know if she was going to live or not—that was one of the worst times for me," said Claire.

For many years, the little white house on Oliver Street has been Claire's home. I asked her what her home means to her. "I love my home. I have been living here sixty-three years. I still love it. Right now, I love the area that was the boys' rooms, where I now watch TV or read my books and my dog Dolly keeps me company. I thank God for every night that I'm here."

At the end of the interview, I had to ask Claire one last question. "Tell me about your vanity that I cherished so much." She stated, "That was our first piece of furniture back in 1945. The little vanity was there when we moved in. I still use it all the time. I think that is where Lani got the idea to have a vanity in her house. I think I sit there more nowadays. I took the little homemade skirt off that Dave made for me. He was a clever man."

As a widow now for many years, Claire enjoys playing cards with her friends and loves to paint by number. As we finished our interview, Claire so easily transitioned to serving us tea, cookies, and vanilla ice cream. As she said, "Now would you like to have tea or coffee?" That was Claire once again taking good care of us with love in her heart.

If it had not been for my best friend Lanette Newman and her loving family, I might not have turned out the way I did. Lanette's mom, Claire, loved each and every one of her five children, and thank God, she had enough love in her heart left for me too. I learned from Lanette's mom the beauty of family values of love, trust, and respect, and allowing everyone to be themselves. There were always a lot of giggles and smiles to go around, and it was a safe place to call my second home.

On June 19, 2010, I was invited to Claire's ninetieth birthday party, held at the Italian American Society Hall on Mission Street in San Francisco. I was prepared to make a brief speech about this special lady, but somehow the cake was served before I could say what I wanted to. Therefore I will write what I wanted to say to her:

> *We are all here tonight to honor a very special lady … my "other" mother, Claire Newman. She is such an inspiration to have reached her ninetieth birthday and to always be so beautiful throughout all her years.*
>
> *I, too, grew up in Daly City, but there was one special home on Oliver Street, where I often played with Cheryl and Lanette. Claire had a special way to always warmly greet you and treat you kindly.*
>
> *Happy ninetieth birthday to you, Claire Newman, my "other" mother—and I wish you many more to come.*

It did not surprise me to discover there is a Saint Clare, born in Assisi in 1194. St. Clare was inspired by the preaching of St. Francis and founded the first women's order of the Franciscans. The "Poor Clares," as they came to be known, won respect for their strict adherence to a life of poverty and soon attracted many followers. Clare herself earned admiration for her devotion to the blessed sacraments, her wise contemplative spirit, the power of her vision, and prayer. Today we can all take inspiration from her life and the humility with which she carried out the work of God (Catholic Church Extension Society, Chicago, IL, Basilica of St. Francis, Assisi, Italy).

"The beauty of a woman is in her soul."
—Author Unknown

INTRODUCING SOUL SISTER LINDA LAKE

As I MENTIONED, I WAS lucky enough for God to send me angels here on earth to help with the challenges of my life. Little did I know that Linda Lake, another neighborhood friend, would in time become my next soul sister. I selected Linda as a soul sister because, through knowing her at a young age, I learned about connecting without judgment, caring and sharing emotional support, and helping each other out in times of challenges through understanding and compassionate listening. Linda is a perfect example of human kindness. She offered to care for my little son without charging me when I was trying desperately to make some positive changes in my life.

Linda helped me when there was nothing for her in it. She demonstrated her kindness and generosity to share what little she had with me at a time when I had nothing to share or give. Linda added a little light and laughter in my dull existence, and for this I will be forever grateful. Through Linda's kindness and helpful actions to me, I learned there was hope for a better tomorrow.

I knew Linda when I was about eight years old or younger. She lived just a few blocks from my house and just across the street from my elementary school, General Pershing School. Maybe that is where I first met her, or was it on one of those days when my mom let me wander off to Linda's neighborhood block? In any event, I liked her right away, though I never guessed our friendship would span some fifty-four years. My first memory of Linda is being at a party at her house celebrating her seventh birthday. I was about a year older at the time. The only memory I have of this party is we kids were sitting in a circle playing for the very first time "Spin the Bottle." All of us little kids sat with our legs outstretched in a circle as the music played in the background, and someone in the circle would lean forward to spin the bottle. I remember the sound of the glass bottle of Coca Cola spinning ever so fast on the wooden floor as we all giggled with excitement. The object of the game is when the bottle stops spinning, you are to kiss the person the bottle is pointing to. I had never played this game before, and the whole topic fascinated me. The kiss for seven- and eight-year-olds was only a peck on the cheek or—if you dared—on the mouth! The other pleasant memory I have about Linda's birthday party was slow dancing with Eddie L. to one of the latest hit songs, "Eddy, My Love." It was sort of neat because I kind of had a crush on Eddie at the time, and to have the song play was just perfect. He was a little gentleman as we danced for the very first time to the music. I thought to myself, *I like this kind of party; this is fun, and it beats "Pin the Tail on the Donkey"!*

Well, years passed, and soon all the kids were in junior high school and then on to high school. Linda and I remained friends, but we sort of drifted apart because she was a seventh grader and I was an eighth grader; it started to make sense to stay within your own age groups, or cliques as others might say. I used to dance a lot with a boy named Stephen in the eighth grade. He was a good dancer and very popular at school. He was never my boyfriend, but we just enjoyed dancing with each other to the good old rock 'n' roll songs of Bobby Darin: "Mack the Knife," "Splish, Splash," and all the others. When the eighth-grade school dance came for all the graduates, Stephen and I danced a lot and at times we won dance contests. I also enjoyed dancing fast with the other popular boys.

Stephen started dating Linda, and I got to see more of her again since they hung out a lot with us at the Hi-Fi Teen Club on Mission Street in Daly City. We would all go to the sock hops and park at "Lake Merced" to watch the "submarine" races and neck with our boyfriends. As the years passed into high school, we started to blend together because some of the boys in my class were now going steady with some of the girls in the class below us, just like Linda and Stephen. Now our parties and high school events included the other kids from other classes, like the juniors and sophomores.

For many of us, it was a secret if we were going steady and things were steaming up a bit. Well, as time passed and before too long, I knew I was pregnant, and so were several other teenage girls in our group. Birth control was unheard of, and we did not have sexual education classes in school—or in the home for that matter. To make a very long story short, Linda and I became teenage mothers well before our time.

It was the summer of 1963 that I got pregnant. My stepfather, in a drunken rage, hit me multiple times one night on the right side of my jaw with his closed fists. By this time, I had had enough of his abusive behavior. I had seen my sister when she was a teenager threaten him one day with a wire hanger if he came any closer to her. He thought twice and backed off and left our bedroom. I had the idea maybe it would work for me too. Only I never counted on how strong he was. As his fists landed on my jaw, I immediately bounced from my bed to the opposite wall, all in one blow from his fists. I slapped him as hard as I could in his face. This went on for some time; I lost count after seventeen times. Finally, my mother for the first time intervened and yelled, "Stop it. You are going to kill her." She went to reach for the pink princess telephone in my bedroom to call the police for help. He ran over and started to pound my mother's hands with his fists. I saw it as my only time to exit the house and leave for anywhere; I would not stay another minute in that crazy house.

Soon after, I discovered I was two months pregnant, penniless, and with no help from my family. My pregnancy was a nightmare, going through hell with my mother, who refused all my phone calls and disowned me for the next three years. My only saving grace was my boyfriend's mother. I was certain she was sent from heaven to care and look after me during this time. I soon began residing at my boyfriend's mother's house. A few months later, my boyfriend was released from a boy's camp for stealing money to help me with the pregnancy. We were married with the permission of a juvenile judge and probation officer. My baby boy was born several months after moving into my mother-in-law's house. My husband's family had roots in New Mexico, and his father was born on an Indian reservation near Gallup, New Mexico. Both his mother and he were born in Santa Fe, New Mexico. I began to learn and discover the cultural differences in households from what I had been used to in food and different styles of cooking. My mother-in-law was making salsa before it replaced catsup on the American table. I remember her cooking pinto beans on the stovetop or, on a special occasion, making menudo soup. She was great at making flour tortillas.

At her house, she spoke Spanish to her friends who came to visit or on the telephone. I remember one day she received a huge burlap bag of dried red chili peppers mailed by her brother in New Mexico. Life was different there, but it was a safe place to have and bring my baby home. My baby's Spanish grandmother loved him and would provide for him until I had a plan to become more independent with or without my husband. He was having trouble taking on the responsibility of being a father and providing for his new family. He did try, but basketball and going out with his friends were high on his list of social activities. It was not long before I began to question whether this was going to work out for both of us and our little baby boy.

It was not until Linda and I both had our baby boys that we met up with each other again. I had heard Linda became pregnant and that she and Stephen were married. She was apparently still living in the house that was her grandmother's in our old neighborhood. Stephen was working at a plumbing company during the week, and on weekends you could usually see him with his head under the hood of their car, trying his hand at being a mechanic. Linda stayed at home raising her baby boy. By the time my baby was ten months old, I was going to night school in San Francisco to be a nurses' aide. I knew I had to earn a living to take care of my baby. His father and I were married, but I realized the obvious: we were both too young to be married with the responsibility of having a family. After one year of married life, I was pretty much living alone in a little studio apartment on Mission Street in Daly City.

During this time, Linda was willing to babysit for me while I was at school. On weekends, if I could, I would go over to Linda's place, and we would sit and talk while our two adorable baby boys played on the kitchen floor together. Thank God we were both blessed with two good little boys who just enjoyed playing together on the linoleum floor in the kitchen while Linda and I chatted away about who knows what. All I know is it was great to be sharing time with someone who was in the same predicament I was in. Little did I know at the time that Linda and I had a very similar childhood, with little attention from our parents and big responsibilities of caring for our siblings. Linda had many little sisters, and I had a younger brother. Much of my responsibility was to watch my little brother and go get him for dinner every day when we went out to play. My brother was the son of my stepfather, which was very lucky for him because he could do no wrong at home. I bonded with my little brother right from the start and wanted to protect him from ever seeing his father in a drunken rage or falling flat on his face after getting out of his car. Linda's story of raising her sisters and protecting them is very similar to mine.

Linda was sweet and kind, and she had a warm smile. She had jet-black long hair and a thin, creamy-white face with pink cheeks; she had a slight build. I liked her a lot and wished I could see more of her, but there was never enough time for someone like me, who had no family for emotional support to help me out. I was the only one in my family who really cared about me or my baby. I was 24-7 a mother, and I can forever recall when my mom said to me, "You made your bed; now you lay in it," as she slammed the phone in my ear.

During this time, Linda was planning a big birthday party for Stephen, and I was looking forward to going. I first had to go to nurses' aide school and then take the Muni Mission No. 14 bus to her house. I was going to arrive late, around ten thirty, but wasn't that when the party was really going to start anyway? I had made a real cute outfit with hip-hugger pants and a shortie top made of green and hot pink flowers. I had cut my hair in a Twiggy haircut, real short with long ball earrings. It was all the rage, and I wanted to fit right in with everyone on the mod "Cher" look, with big eyes of mascara and eyeliner.

I had been keeping my eye on a fellow that I would see whenever I went to Linda's house. His name was John, and he had no idea I had a big crush on him. Going to Linda's party would be a great time to let him know I had eyes for him, so I was really ready to party when I walked in on the house full of partygoers. I was right, the party was going full steam ahead, and I could tell everyone was having a good time dancing and drinking a little. My plan to sweep John off his feet came crumbling down when I realized he had come with a date. I felt real downhearted, and then something came over me—I do not know whether it was the music to "My Guy" or "You Beat Me to the Punch," I found myself telling John I needed to see him outside because I wanted to tell him something. Once outside with John, I shared with him about my plan to be with him at the party tonight and how I was so surprised to see him with his date. He laughed and said, "Well, okay" as he kissed me under the stars on a warm summer night. After that night, John and I were an item for several months. I was forever grateful to Linda for having the party; it was perfect timing.

This was the era of "sex, drugs, and rock 'n' roll." It was 1967 when Linda and went our separate ways in life. We grew up in a time when San Francisco and Daly City were impacted by the antiwar protests, the sexual revolution, and the women's rights movement, and so too were our lives. The song "San Francisco (Be Sure to Wear Flowers in Your Hair)" by Scott McKenzie was all the rage. I went on to get my medical assistant certificate and became employed with Kaiser Permanente Medical Program in San Francisco.

I often thought about Linda, and one day just about five years ago, I received a phone call when living in Vacaville, California. When the soft voice on the phone said, "Is this Susan Freire?" I said, "Yes," not knowing who it was, and then she said, "Well, it better be because I just spent $50.00 to get your phone number." It was like all the years faded away between us as we talked on the phone with each other. I found out that Linda was now living in Oregon. We wasted no time making plans to meet each other again in San Francisco.

It was a windy night in San Francisco when Linda and I and both our husbands met for the first time. Linda and Allen had made reservations in a penthouse in San Francisco, and we were on top of the hotel balcony sharing stories, laughs, and drinks as the night fell on the city. It was as if no time had passed. Sure, we both looked older, and I a little fatter, and Linda a little thinner, but there we were just looking at each other, smiling like we had done so many times before. I was back in the city on the rooftop with all the neighbor houses so close together, and I could see the city lights starting to turn off as the neighborhood prepared for bed. As we left Linda and Allen, we made plans to meet again. Driving home, I shared all kinds of stories with my husband, and I had this wonderful, warm feeling going through my body of meeting an old friend and knowing we had shared something that was very special during one of the most difficult and painful times in our lives. Thank you, soul sister Linda, for being there for me when my young life was in shambles.

Linda and I were raised in a time of the affluent 1950s; however, child abuse, child neglect, and child abandonment were the cultural norm for us. We went into domestic violence relationships with our young husbands, and our lives were forever affected by this exposure. There were no support groups, women's shelters, or places to expose the secrets of what was really going on in our homes and lives. It was a time when you were on your own to make do as best you could and to have the strength and courage to continue on when all hope seemed lost.

It is important to understand that the 1960s and 1970s were defining a new counterculture of sex, drugs, and rock 'n' roll. Life was confusing for me at this time because I identified myself as a Catholic who knew only about abuse, confessionals, and penance. Now in the 1960s, all the values and beliefs we learned as children in religion classes had fallen to the wayside. Now you did not have to worry about kissing on the first date; it was okay to go to bed on the first date if you wanted. There was no worry about smoking because everyone was turning on and lighting up with weed and other drugs, which were all new for the day.

As a generation, we were defining a new normal for our lifestyles. I did not choose at this time to use drugs because I was focused on getting ahead and having a better life for myself and my baby son. Unfortunately, my husband and lots of others got caught up in the new trends that would change their lives forever.

It was a time when everyone was fighting for their rights. There were civil rights, women's rights, human rights, and much more, it was a time of turbulence with the Vietnam War and college students in unrest about these changing times.

Having set the stage for this time period, here is Linda's incredible life story and her struggle through the eras of the 1950s and the 1960s as she knew them, and the wonderful outcome of being a complete woman with an open heart.

"FROM HAND TO HAND AND HEART TO HEART"
by Linda Lake

"MY LIFE STORY. HMMMMM. I guess I'll start with what I've been told and by sharing memories that have undoubtedly been shaped by my personal experience."

"Barbara, your mother needs you. She's in trouble again." The little girl slowly rises from her desk, lowers her head, and tries to ignore the catcalls and taunts from her classmates. Humiliated, her shoulders hunched over and rigid, fighting back tears that threaten to overtake her and never stop, she trudges down the steps of the school to go and find her mother, Nona. Once again, Nona has passed out, drunk, on the street. My mother finds her, helps her struggle to her feet, tries to wipe the vomit from the front of her dress, and helps her onto the bus to take her home.

My mother was born into an alcoholic family, and as a female born between two brothers, she was responsible for taking care of everyone. Her father turned a blind eye to his wife's behavior and relied on my mother to hold the family together. Additionally, he was very strict. He once forbade my mother, who was dressed and ready to go to the prom, from leaving the house. I am not sure why. When the story was relayed to me, I couldn't believe he was acting strictly out of meanness. He must have been angry about something. Perhaps he needed to control her. He certainly couldn't control his wife. His wife, Nona, would often go to the store for a pack of cigarettes and not return for several weeks, or until her husband, Joe, tracked her down and brought her back home.

Because Nona's alcoholic behaviors had mellowed by the time I was born, I was spared much of the public humiliation my mother was forced to endure. Although one of my jobs within the family was to entertain the disheartened adults with whom I lived, I was basically responsible only for myself. Mom got pregnant with me when she was sixteen. I was born when she was seventeen years of age—one of her patterns I would later repeat. On my birth certificate, she listed herself as eighteen years old. I am not sure why, but as I discovered while writing this story, there were many half-truths and secrets that were kept from me. My father, or the man who is listed on my birth certificate, was madly in love with her. I know this because he went against his family's wishes and married her. In the pictures I've seen of them together, you can clearly see he's smitten. She, on the other hand, looks as if she's in a fog and about to cry.

After my mother and father married, they moved in with his recently widowed mother, Betty. She hated my mother and treated her very badly. She doubted that her only, beloved son, Jimmy, was the father of the bastard baby that was on the way. She ridiculed my mother, had her do all of the housework (never done to her satisfaction, of course), and turned her son against his young wife by constantly making stupid and false accusations, for example, blaming my mother for tearing the curtains when it was obvious the dog had done it. She asked Johnny over and over again how he could be sure he was the father. After all, Barbara lived in a rundown house, her mother was a drunk, and there was that group of boys always hanging around. How could he be so sure it was his? In the beginning, he didn't listen. After a while, he turned on my mother and also began to attack her. Their marriage was doomed to fail. For some reason, I was not allowed to live with my mother and father in Sacramento. I was told it had something to do with money, but I always felt there was some other reason. I surmised it was because I wasn't good enough or pretty enough to be loved.

I lived with my mother's parents in Daly City, a two-hour drive south from Sacramento. Nona (I called her by her first name) was tall, slim, and graceful and a wonderful listener. She had a great sense of humor and was very intelligent. Even in her drunken haze, Nona would listen to me. With eyes glazed and swaying from side to side while holding an imported cigarette, she'd stand for hours while I'd go on and on about my daily trials and tribulations. She would patiently nod while I struggled to understand the world around me. What an affirming experience! By listening and letting me figure things out for myself, she was telling me I was smart and that she had faith in me.

I didn't find out until after Nona's death that she had been an accomplished piano player. I wonder how many of her talents were sublimated as she became a wife and mother. Was her need to drink herself into a stupor every night (except Sunday) driven by a need to mask the pain brought about by having to ignore her creative side? Women of her generation had so few options. You got married and had children. That was it. Nona had three children and did her best to cope.

Many years later, my mother, Nona, and I had a rare opportunity to sit and talk to each other without interruption. Nona and my mother were drinking their wine, and I was smoking a joint. I was in my mid-thirties so they knew I smoked pot, and by this time they had no judgments against it. I am not sure how the subject came up, but Nona told us that she had once given herself an abortion. She described how she took a coat hanger and jammed it up into her cervix until she started to bleed profusely and miscarried. Nona then excused herself and left the room, leaving my mother and me to contemplate what she had shared. We looked at each other, not sure what to say, and sat for a few minutes in silence. My mother swallowed hard and went on to tell me of an incident that happened when she was a child. She came home one day and found Nona lying on the couch, bleeding and very sick. She had to call a cab to take her mother to the hospital. She was not sure at the time what was wrong, but now she put the pieces together. She told me Nona was the kind of woman who should never have married. Nona didn't have a voice in the matter, so she drank instead and almost killed herself rather than face the prospect of having another child.

Even with all the anguish that was passed from generation to generation, my family still found time to laugh and find humor in their world. I was told that before Nona started working full-time, she would amuse herself and those around her with Lucille Ball-type antics. Whenever she got a new dish or appliance, she would gather all the children, march to the backyard, and throw the "old" item up against the back fence and break it! Everyone would cheer and be delighted with the ceremony, except the people next door who would look over their beautifully manicured yard into our yard filled with an odd assortment of dishes, toasters, irons, and such in the midst of overgrown blackberry bushes.

Nona did not tolerate any form of racism or bigotry. If anyone made a racial slur (like when my grandfather ridiculed Asians for their driving skills), they were told in no uncertain terms that that behavior was not acceptable and would not be tolerated. I learned from her and my mother that all people were the same and stereotyping was ignorant and immoral. In the 1950s, as my mother, grandmother, grandfather, and I watched the civil rights demonstrations on television, I'd become angry. It scared me! I recall starting to cry and shouting, "Why can't someone just go down there, stand on a box, and tell those people to just stop it?" I couldn't understand how people could treat others so horribly. The dogs! The violence! The children crying! My mother explained to me that "they" (the Southern white people) didn't see Negroes as human and felt they could do anything they wanted to them. I was perplexed and mortified. *We* knew all people were the same and did our best to ignore color lines. Those white people on television were mean, stupid, and bad.

In the very early 1960s, the topic of legalized abortions was being discussed in the media and in Congress. I was in junior high school at the time and was ambivalent about whether abortions should be legal. I asked my mother, and she said, "You will never stop abortions. Legalizing them will only stop desperate women from dying in back alleys from botched operations." Her statement made a big impact on me and helped shape my political views regarding *Roe vs. Wade*. Years later, when the reversal of the law was being considered, I marched with thousands of people demanding the law not be changed. I did not want the government telling me what I could and could not do with my body. Also, I saw the repeal of the law as a step backward for women's rights. I wear the label of a feminist proudly and will do my best to make sure the struggle is not forgotten.

My grandfather was my life. He let me cuddle up next to him on the couch. I'd tell him stories, and he'd smile down at me with a look of pure delight in his eyes. His body was warm and comfy, he smelled like Brylcreem, and he had thinning hair that he folded over his forehead and a small round belly that I used to rest my head upon. He made me feel safe. I was the love of his life, and I knew it.

Because he had no teeth, or very few, he seldom smiled. That made him look incredibly stern, and all my friends were afraid of him. Nevertheless, I knew he was my protector. No one would mess with me and risk being the object of his wrath. One time an older boy pushed me off the side of a hill that was supported by a cement wall. It was probably no more than two feet high, but I fell and skinned my knee. I ran home crying and told my Dada, "Stanley pushed me off the hill!" Dada followed me back to the scene of the crime, found Stanley, and warned him never to hurt me again. Stanley was afraid, and I was glad. As Dada and I walked away, I looked back over my shoulder, put my nose in the air, mumbled, "Hurumph," and went home, flipping my ponytail from side to side. *That will teach you a thing or two,* I thought smugly to myself. Stanley never bothered me again, nor did any of the other boys. The funny thing was that Dada was the most gentle man you could find. Little children adored him and would climb all over him when he was available. It was only the scallywags that messed with me that got his dander up. And they deserved it!

I was happy in my loving grandparents' home. Because I didn't know anything else, having this elusive young woman, my mother, come and go from my life seemed natural. When my mother and Gary lived in Sacramento, she used to "sneak" money (he was very tight and held the purse strings) and take the bus to San Francisco to visit me. I have a beautiful picture of her, as a young woman, holding me tightly in her arms. She is sitting on the ground in the middle of our overgrown, weed-infested yard with a scarf around her head. She is looking intently at this funny-looking baby in her arms—me! For so many years, I thought she didn't love me, but looking at this picture, you can't deny the mother/child bond. My mother finally left my father when I was about two years old. I don't remember what reason my mother gave for leaving, but I vaguely recall something about money and Gary's unwillingness to support me or pay for my mother's visits to me. Whatever it was, I knew from an early age that I must not have been very important to my father. What was wrong with me? Why didn't he love me?

My father Gary appeared without warning when I was about five years old. Although I had never seen him, I knew who he was the minute I opened the door. Looking up at this handsome stranger, who looked very much like Paul Newman with a James Dean haircut, I told him, "My mother's not here." He replied with a smile, "I didn't come to see her. I came to see you." He took me to Playland at the Beach (an amusement park in San Francisco), and we went on the faster, adult rides that scared me to death. I bit my lip, tried to hide my fear, and pretended I was having fun. He must have noticed my clenched teeth, eyes popping out of my head, and knuckles turning white from holding onto the safety bar for dear life. I remember him looking down at me and chuckling as my skinny little body bounced all over the roller-coaster car, my face looking as if I was in a wind tunnel. "Are you having fun, Linda?" he asked with a menacing grin. *Sure, you jerk. I enjoy being thrown about mercilessly by a piece of gyrating metal that threatens to fling me to the ground, run over me, and decapitate me.* He eventually took me home and left with little fanfare. The vertebrae that popped in my back as I was being thrashed about on our "fun time" together still bothers me to this day.

By the time I started school, being pretty was very important to me. Before my mother married her second husband, I would lie on my bed and watch her get dressed for a date. It was quite a process. She was very beautiful—akin to Ava Gardner. Strangely enough, she always seemed more at ease and content when she was single. I remember asking her if I was pretty, and she said, "No. You're not really pretty, but you're the type of girl who will make men stop and stare." I didn't know what that meant, but I knew I wanted to be pretty. Like my mother. And she said I wasn't.

My mother remarried when I was about six. I met Charles for the first time when my mother took me to their house. He was a big man who never really looked at me. Needless to say, he and I never hit it off. He was never mean to me or anything. In fact, he never said a word to me or looked in my direction. He just totally ignored me. They moved into a house around the corner from me and my grandparents. My first little sister, Lia, was born soon after. She had her own room in the house with my mother and new husband. Why couldn't I live with my mother like Lia? Again, I assumed it was because I wasn't good enough or pretty enough. Lia was adorable—everything I was not. She had big, blue eyes; thick, long, dark eyelashes; silky blonde hair with flecks of gold running through it; a pixie nose; and a perfect bowlike mouth that would later turn into a seductive pout. On the other hand, when I looked in the mirror, I saw the television comedian Sid Caesar! He had a mole on his cheek just like I did! I certainly couldn't compete with Lia. My hair was always out of control, I was skinny, and I had knobby knees. My nose was too big. *And* My mom had already told me I wasn't pretty! No wonder I couldn't live with them. This cute little baby was better than me. Oh, well. I had perfected the "It doesn't matter" attitude by the time Lia was born. I had learned to stifle my feelings and disregard my thoughts. Although that served me well as a child, as an adult, I had trouble identifying my true sentiment and found it difficult to be authentic.

Lia was my first sister and the first to be subjected to my ambivalence, impatience, and animosity. Although I acted as if I couldn't care less, I loved her dearly and still do. Although nonchalant and aloof, I became very protective of her. Later, when my other sisters came along, I did my best to shield them from the troubles they were experiencing at home and give them as much of myself as I could. Alas, being a child myself, I was not up to the task of nurturing them, which is what they really needed. I blamed myself for not being able to help them more and carried that guilt around with me for years.

I visited my mother and her new husband (Lia's father) on the weekends. That was my first indoctrination to domestic violence. While they were in the bedroom, I would lie on the couch and listen to him beat her. I curled up in a ball and cried and cried. One time when he left the house after a beating, my mother tried to comfort me. I yelled through my tears that the next time he was hurting her, I was going to run into the bedroom and tell him, "Stop hurting my mother!" She smiled at my naiveté and told me that would only make things worse. I wanted to help her, and I couldn't. I never said anything about what was going on to anyone, not even to my grandparents. My bouts with asthma, which plagued me since I was eighteen months old, became more frequent, and my chest often ached from trying not to cry while gasping for breath.

When my mother finally got the nerve to leave Lia's father, she and Lia joined me at my grandparents' house. Unfortunately, that served only as a temporary refuge. One day when I returned from school, I found the adults buzzing around and whispering. The back door had been kicked in. Charles now knew where we were, and we had to get away, fast. We threw a few things in the car and headed out, escaping in the middle of the night. While our car was driving down the hill on the way out of town, we saw his car driving up the hill toward us. I was instructed to get down and hide. We all held our breaths, and somehow he missed us and drove on by.

We went to stay with friends in Stockton. Once there, I was told to stay away from the windows (the curtains were constantly drawn) and was seldom allowed outside. One night, when I was supposed to be asleep, I heard my mother say she was afraid he was going to find and hurt us. Needless to say,

I couldn't sleep that night. I kept seeing him in the shadows and coped with the situation by pretending we were all acting in a television drama. My make-believe world saved me from danger. As an adult, I used that technique to give me some semblance of control whenever threatened.

Eventually it was determined that we were out of immediate danger, and we returned to my grandparents' house. I continued to feel anxious and worried. I bit my nails until they bled, and my mind continued to play "What if?" every night. I don't recall any significant events related to my mother and Lia returning to my grandparents' house other than our two-bedroom house was now accommodating five people from three generations. My mother slept on a roll-away bed in the dining room, and Lia's crib was in the bedroom with Dada. I must have slept in my grandmother's room.

I continued to excel academically, was well liked, and took refuge in the structure provided by my teachers. My circle of friends began to grow, and I was happy. By this time, I had become pretty independent. Every morning I'd get myself up, fix my lunch, and wake my mother so she could put my hair in a ponytail before I headed to school. When I got older and was still mad at my mother, I'd dredge up this memory to make her feel guilty and me feel righteous. I wasted so much time being angry with her. She had her own psychological impairments, and she was doing the best she could. Years later, when I was finally ready to let go of the anger that masked my pain for so long and allow the love my mother had for me to become tangible, everything in my life changed. My heart, which had been constricted and constrained by resentment, opened and relaxed. My passage through life became easier and clearer.

Two years after my mother's separation from Charles and her return to my grandparents' house, I came home from school and was told by my babysitter that I had a new little sister. What? How did that happen? My mother had hid her pregnancy, and no one knew she was carrying a baby until she went into early labor, at seven and a half months, and almost died. She had placenta-previa and had to have several blood transfusions. Those details were kept hidden from me, and I couldn't figure out how a new baby suddenly popped into our lives. No preparations had been made for a new baby, so when my mother and Eileen came home, Eileen had to sleep in a drawer. She was so tiny that she fit in her makeshift bassinette perfectly. Eileen's appearance did not upset me like Lia's arrival had because I had developed a strong support group at school. I'd look down at this little life and ask, "Where did you come from? How did you get here?" I had been told babies came with married couples, and my mother wasn't married. Hmmmm.

Evidently my mother had attempted a brief reconciliation with Lia's father, resulting in her pregnancy with Eileen. He had tried to win her back with promises of being a changed man. I was told he drank the last milk in the house and ate the last egg, leaving nothing for the baby. My mother saw he was still the self-centered, selfish, and very dangerous, crazy man he had always been. She left, bringing Lia home to live with me and my grandparents. Although Eileen was an unexpected addition to our family, she grew to become a very important part of our family's cohesiveness. I felt a special connection with her. She had no father, she was skinny with pale white skin, and she kind of looked like me. As she became older, it was obvious she was smart, funny, and caring (almost to a fault). Everybody loved her, but I don't think she believed it. She wore her heart on her sleeve, and unfortunately she turned to alcohol in an attempt to fill her emptiness.

My mother had started dating a man she had known for years. He was the younger brother of her best friend. He was very handsome, blond with blue eyes, drove a cute little sports car, and wore saddle shoes and cardigan sweaters. They fell in love, and my mother was on to her third marriage. As she didn't know the whereabouts of her second husband (we heard he was in jail), she filed for and was granted a Mexican divorce. My world changed significantly when my mother remarried. Although I had to move away from my friends and my grandparents' house, I consoled myself with the fact that I was with my mother and I had my own room. I felt pretty special. I had a space of my own in a three-bedroom house that soon had to accommodate six children.

My mother seemed more peaceful after she and Jim married. She'd sit and knit with a slight, almost secretive, smile on her face. If I remember correctly, she even began to hum! She was the happiest I had ever seen her. I don't know how I knew, but I figured out she was pregnant. When she confirmed my suspicions, I was ecstatic. A little baby doll to play with! Of course, I didn't realize the danger she was in by having another baby. She had been warned by the doctor after Eileen's harrowing birth not to have any more children. It could kill her. She ignored the advice and went ahead, handling her pregnancy as if she didn't have a care in the world.

Elizabeth was adorable. She had wavy blonde hair, a precious little nose, and big blue eyes. She was extremely good-natured. I don't recall her ever crying. I remember watching her as a toddler, wobbling around the house quietly, trying to figure out her world. I loved her bubbly personality and bouncy blonde curls. Just looking at her made me smile and feel good inside. When I picked her up and made her giggle, I was in heaven.

By the time I reached the age of twelve, I was still tall and skinny. I had no hint of boobs nor my period. I used to stand on the bathroom scale and grumble every time I saw it register less than a hundred pounds. My mother used to laugh, knowing that I would eventually be grateful for having a high metabolism and being able to eat a hot fudge sundae every day for a week and not gain an ounce. (That changed, of course, after the birth of my first child.)

I became aware that something was changing right before my thirteenth birthday. I was standing at the bottom of the steps in my polka-dot capris, with a long ponytail and a scarf tied around my neck. I thought I was pretty cool and looked like one of the girls in the Archie comic books. A boy in a car drove by and whistled at me! I flipped my ponytail to the other side and sighed nonchalantly. My heart was pounding so that I was sure he could hear it. I felt giggly, proud, and confused. Is this what my mother was talking about? I certainly wasn't pretty, but a boy whistled at me. I must have something!

Unfortunately, not long after Elizabeth's birth, I was hit with prepuberty angst. I was confused about what was going on in my body and had incredible mood swings. I felt frightened and didn't know why. I tried to find my place in this different, ever-expanding family, and felt totally alone. My new world was so different from the one I was familiar with. I no longer had my grandfather to cuddle with, or my grandmother to listen to me and offer reassuring words. My friends lived several miles away, and now there was this man in the house who my mother flitted around while ignoring me. I became sullen and then angry. At times, poor little Elizabeth took the brunt of my resentment and unpredictable rage (as did all my sisters, I am sure).

My mother once again became pregnant not long after Elizabeth's birth. I was mortified and very worried. We were having financial problems, and I knew instinctively, even at fourteen years of age, that we could not afford another baby. We were already drinking powdered milk, and the portions at the dinner table were getting smaller and smaller. When I learned of the pregnancy, I remember yelling at my mother, "How can we feed another kid?" and stomping out of the room. I was right, of course, but my mother could do nothing about it, and it was none of my business. Abortions were not legal nor part of her character. One time when all of us sisters questioned her on the wisdom of having six children, she yelled back at us, "Which one of you should I have aborted?" All of us quickly shut up. Birth control was available, and I always wondered why she didn't take more precautions. I now theorize that having so many children was her way of solidifying her marriage. How could he leave her if she had six kids? Also, having so many children ensured that she would always have someone to care for and love.

Kate was born eleven months after Elizabeth. This time my mother didn't sit around knitting with a smile. This time she had that "deer in the headlights" look and stood around shaking her hands if she was trying to fling some invisible bits of dread from her fingers. What made this pregnancy even more difficult was the fact my mother contracted German measles at the end of her third month. The ensuing six months were undoubtedly filled with worries about whether the baby was going to be okay and whether she would make it through another delivery. At the end of the ninth month, she called me into the bathroom, trembling. The floor was covered with blood. She shoved a few towels in my hand and instructed me to clean up the blood before the girls saw it. It is the one time I remember looking straight into each other's eyes, with no distractions, embarrassment, or shame. We connected on a primal level, woman to woman. No other words were said. I did what I was told, and she went to call her husband. I returned to my room, shut the door, sat on the bed, and began to shake my hands just like I had seen my mother do when she was extremely anxious. Although I tried not to consider the perilous possibilities, I played my "What if?" game late into the night and for several nights thereafter. What if my mother died? What if the baby was deformed? What if it's my fault for being such a brat and worrying my mother to distraction?

My mother and sister made it through the delivery, but there was little relief when the baby came home. My mother was okay, but poor Kate cried all the time. And I mean *all* the time! Nothing my distressed mother did could calm the baby down, and I refused to go near that howling, scrawny, wiggly thing. I was such a selfish teenager. I did little to help my mother or the family. I had learned to observe the family without really participating. I was on the sidelines, looking in with disdain. Although I loved my mother and my sisters, this was *not* how I thought my life was supposed to be.

My new stepfather was now drinking a fifth of vodka every day. Every morning he'd fill a large tumbler full of the clear poison and down it like it was a glass of milk. As his alcoholism became more and more predominant, he began to abuse my sisters more and more often. My mother refused to stand up to him and protect the children. He used to scream at them, especially the two-year-old, Kate. He would call her stupid and clumsy, which of course made her start to shake and spill her milk. He'd stand behind this sweet, cherub-faced, little towhead, swaying in his drunken stupor, heaping abuse and insults down upon the little girl. Her little face would turn bright red, her eyes would water, and she'd start to gag and would eventually vomit. I never saw her cry.

He said he had a "personality conflict" with Kate. How an adult can have a personality conflict with a two-year-old is beyond me. I'd look to my mother, expecting her to do something. Seeing her lost in denial behind her newspaper, I'd finally grab the baby and take her from the table. "How can you let him talk to her like that?" I'd scream. My mother, totally ignoring the chaos, would say nothing.

My last sister was born a year after Kate. Being the youngest of six, it must have been difficult for Stephanie to have her needs met. She was, and is, beautiful and very smart. Because of her intellect and her fierce determination, she found a way through the chaos and has gone on to be very successful professionally.

With all the commotion brought about by having six children, my mother was oblivious to my pain. Or, if she did notice, she chose to pay no attention. I felt as if I was hurtling down a dark tunnel, bombarded by conflicting feelings and images. My grades began to slip, and I started to have suicidal fantasies. By cutting myself and screaming at my baby sisters, I was begging for someone to see my pain and help me. No one did.

By my sophomore year, my grades continued to go down (especially in algebra, in which I had always excelled), and I began to daydream in class. I began thinking about when I would be able to escape the dreary life in which I found myself. When I'd go to my grandparents' house to visit, I'd sit in the dark and look out the window watching the San Francisco skyline. Lost in melancholia, I'd dream of a life free of violence and unhappiness. I was determined to get away and make a happier life for myself. I just didn't know how I'd do it.

Evidently I started to get a cute figure, because boys started to treat me differently. It made me blush, but I liked it. I was fourteen and had two boyfriends, Steve and Russell. I asked my mother whom she thought I should go with, and she recommended Steve. She thought I'd have more fun with him. So, Russell became a thing of the past, and I started having "fun" with Steve, especially in the backseat of his friend's car and in his room with the door shut.

There was no birth control available for us, so Steve and I played Russian roulette, with little thought about me getting pregnant. Steve used the withdraw method, and that worked for a while. Then we got careless, and I got pregnant. Looking back at it now, perhaps I subconsciously wanted to get pregnant as a way out of my dismal home life. When I finally faced the fact that I was, indeed, pregnant, my immature mind thought I would find the love I was longing for by having a baby and marrying my adoring boyfriend. Abortion never entered our minds. It was illegal in those days, and all you heard was horror stories of the botched, back-alley operations. All Steve and I knew was we *had* to get married. To his credit, he never wavered in his decision, and I never doubted for a minute that he would marry me. After all, we were in love.

After I had missed four menstrual cycles, my body began to change. I became very voluptuous (my boobs looked great!), and I briefly enjoyed my newfound curves. People began to notice, including my mother. One morning, right before my senior year was about to start, while sitting at the breakfast table with my pants unzipped because they were too tight, I asked my mother when I could go shopping for school clothes. She left the room in a huff, yelling over her shoulder, "How are you going to fit into them?" She knew.

Arrangements for a hasty marriage were made, and a ceremony was performed in the living room of a dilapidated house in San Francisco's Tenderloin District. Our wedding gifts were $20 from his parents and enough Blue Chip Stamps to buy a hand mixer from mine. Once at the motel, we were so scared and unfamiliar with what we were supposed to do except consummate our marriage that we couldn't sleep all night for fear we'd sleep past the 11:00 a.m. checkout time and be put in jail! I do have one sweet memory. Steve got out of bed and began to write me a letter, professing his love for me and his confidence in our future. I smiled at him and asked him to come back to bed. I regret not letting him complete the letter because there are so few memories of our young love. At that moment, however, we both were sure we'd be together forever.

Steve and I had no place to live and could not afford an apartment. He had a job but was only earning minimum wage. My parents let him use an old jalopy we had to drive down to see me after work while we continued to live apart. The one rule was that we could never go into my room together and shut the door. So, even though we were legally married, we were not allowed to be alone. My mother didn't want us having sex under her roof. We lived this way (with occasional makeout sessions in the car or across the street under the high school football stands) until my grandfather died two months later and it was decided we would move into my grandmother's house. Steve never saw me naked until I was big and fat and seven months pregnant.

My grandfather had had cancer, and somehow it was determined that it was in my best interest not to tell me how sick he was. Before he died, my mother told me it was lucky he was so ill and didn't notice I was pregnant because if he had known, it would have killed him. Not long after she said that, he died. It still hurts my heart when I think I only made one visit to the hospital to see him. I hid my pregnancy under my well-worn, old coat and held in my stomach. We talked a bit. I tried to feed him, but he was in too much pain to eat. Dada, a very private person, was lined up against the wall with the other patients and had no privacy. I knew he must have been mortified by his lack of dignity, but he was too sick to do anything about it. My heart ached for him. When we got the call in the middle of the night that he had died, another part of my world fell apart. My whole being began to cry, quietly, from way deep inside. He loved me unconditionally and gave me comfort, reassurance, and protection. I knew he would always be there for me, and now he was gone. Here I was, sixteen, pregnant, married, and scared to death. Even though I had a husband, I felt totally alone. Since Dada died, I have never been able to fill the empty space in my heart. I was not allowed to go to his funeral (not that I wanted to) because my mother thought it would upset me too much and I might lose the baby. I have not visited his grave, and the sadness I feel when I think of him reminds me I am still grieving.

Not long after Steve was professing his love for me, he began abusing me, just as his father had done to his mother. I was scared and confused and couldn't believe the man who had said he loved me wanted to hurt me so. I disregarded his hateful behavior and, just like my mother, hid in a world of denial. As I had no role models to help define my new identity, I turned to the perfect television mother and wife, Donna Reed. She was pretty, kept a clean house, was married to a handsome man who loved her dearly, and always knew just what to say and do. I decided that was the kind of wife/mother I was going to be. Unfortunately, I did not have any of Donna Reed's skills. No matter how I tried, I couldn't keep the house clean, and my culinary skills were nonexistent. I bought cabbage for dinner, thinking it was lettuce, my pork chops were stringy and tough, and I put my husband's underwear in the wash with a pink blanket and turned everything pink. Many times, my young husband would pick up his dinner plate, throw it against the wall (just as his father had done), and scream obscenities at me. I'd clean up the mess, head down, not saying a word, knowing he was right. As much as I wanted to please him, I knew I was a failure.

I was fat and lonely, and my "adoring" husband was seldom at home. When he was home, I was mostly ridiculed or ignored. Still, I continued to get up every morning before he did, put on my makeup, and warm his underwear by the heater. I wanted to paint a blissful domestic picture, but the dreamlike colors I used as a cover couldn't hide the deception I was living with for very long. Steve, who was often unemployed, was rarely home. I felt deserted and isolated. The many friends I had in high school no longer called. I sat day after day in my dark, dusty house, eating avocados, watching *General Hospital* on television, and trying to ignore my sorrow. One morning while I was putting away my high school yearbooks, I began to cry. I never made it to my senior year. My son would never know how popular I was. My claims to fame had been obliterated, and the accolades I received in school were no longer relevant. I put the yearbooks in the back of my cluttered closet, shut the door, and pretended it didn't matter.

Two weeks after my due date, my water broke. I called Steve at the local bar, and he came right home. He sat nervously as I put on my makeup and combed my hair. I was very calm and collected, sure I could handle what was about to happen. I called my mother, certain she would want to be with me and witness the birth of her first grandchild. She told me she was not going to come. "There is really nothing I can do, so have Steve call me when it's over," she said. What? My mother didn't want to be with me? Was she punishing me? Was she so busy with her other children that I didn't matter? Or did she really just not care? I was crushed but brushed it off as no big deal.

Steve and I drove calmly to the hospital, and as we entered the door, my first real contraction hit. What was this? I tried that puffing and puffing thing I read about in my borrowed pregnancy library books, and it wasn't helping! Yikes! This was not what I anticipated. I was clumsily transferred to a cold, steel gurney and tied down to make the job easier for the doctor. The restraints were so tight I had to ask the nurse to please scratch my nose. All of a sudden, there was confusion, concerned voices, and people bustling about. The air became thick with a purple mist as my baby was being born breeched! His little butt was coming first! If the doctor couldn't get the baby's head out quickly, there could be serious problems. The doctor forgot about me and began to pull at and twist my little boy, struggling to release him from my body. After a few moments, he was free, and his ferocious crying let us all know he had made it. Except for some gas I was given as Joey was heading down the birth canal, I used no drugs. Because I was clear-headed and drug free, the instant he was born, I felt like Superwoman! I could move tall buildings! I was in touch with the heavens! I was capable of anything! I had made a human being!

I asked if Joey could be brought to me. I wanted him with me all the time. They moved his bassinette into my room so he was always within reach. After the drama subsided, I reached for my son. At that moment, he became the center of my universe. As the years went by, no matter what I was doing or how distracted I seemed to be, there was a piece of my heart reserved for Joey and Joey alone. That continues today, even as he heads toward his forty-fifth birthday. Holding my baby, looking down at his reddish, round face, I immediately fell in love. Poor little guy. He undoubtedly had been traumatized by the birth experience. They yanked him from my womb, where he had snuggled safely for nine and a half months, grabbed him by the heels, held him upside down, stretched his spine, and slapped him on his bottom. No mercy. His introduction to this world was not gentle. Now, as an adult, his spirit screams out, "Hold me!" but his persona demonstrates a gruffness that continues to guard his tender soul. It's only when you look in his eyes or sit with him in silence that you can feel the pain behind his bravado. He is afraid to show his gentleness. He has been taught by his father that being gentle does not go along with being a man.

When I was allowed to hold my baby, my heart felt as if it would burst. I had never before experienced that overwhelming, all-encompassing feeling of love. I would hold him, tightly, and let him sleep on my chest. I had never

41

seen anything so beautiful nor loved anything so much. I still get angry when I remember the stern nurse, with a thick German accent, who came into my room and scolded me for holding my baby too long. She said I was going to spoil him. At seventeen and not sure what was right, I listened to her and put my baby back in the bassinette. My body ached to hold him, and late at night, when no one was around, I'd sneak him into my bed and listen to him breathe. When we got Joey home, I discovered he would only sleep on my chest. Spoiling him indeed! I was going to hold my baby!

I finished high school by attending adult school at night. Girls who were pregnant were not allowed to attend school in the day. They were a bad influence on the other girls. I was mortified when I was in night school one night and my breasts started to leak when it was time to feed Joey. I pretended nothing was happening as my shirt became more and more wet, drenched with milk that was meant for my son. Ignoring my embarrassment, I kept my focus. I stayed in school and graduated.

Whereas the emotional abuse began as soon as Steve and I started living together, the physical violence didn't start until after Joey was born. It breaks my heart to remember Steve hitting me on the leg, over and over, as Joey watched, hanging onto the side of his crib, crying. On one occasion, Steve, Joey, and I were driving across the Golden Gate Bridge, and Steve threatened to stop the car and throw Joey and me over the side. I just sat there, holding my son tightly in my arms, and waited for his threats to subside. Although Steve never abused Joey physically (that was something I could not have ignored), he continually teased and ridiculed his son. I used to beg Steve to stop, telling him he was going to make Joey insecure. Steve ignored my pleas, and Joey grew up doubting himself and sabotaging any successes that came his way. Nevertheless, he continues to adore his father and continues to seek his transitory approval.

I was nineteen years old when I decided I wanted another baby. My Donna Reed fantasy kept me from seeing things as they really were. I lived for the times when Steve was nice to me and held onto those fleeting moments, as seldom as they were, as proof that our marriage was okay. My dear friend Colette tried to warn me that having another baby was a huge mistake. She felt by having another child, I'd be stuck in a world of unhappiness and poverty. I refused to believe her prediction and blindly went ahead. Steve and I agreed another baby would be "fun," and I happily skipped to the bathroom and flushed my birth control pills down the toilet.

I was thrilled when I got pregnant. I watched my diet, felt great, and looked forward to having a new friend to share my life with. I believed I had Joey for Steve, and this new baby would be for me. Steve still continued to spend his evenings out with "friends." I turned a blind eye to my suspicions and ignored his absence, along with the phone numbers in his pocket and makeup on his shirt. I just couldn't believe he would be unfaithful. Through it all, I still thought he loved me.

By the time William was born in 1968, the medical profession had changed its approach to childbirth. It was much less barbaric. As a result, William's birth was much easier. I was not strapped down, the doctor seemed to be in tune with my needs, and they actually invited the father into the delivery room! When Steve was given the option of attending the birth, he took a step backward, gulped down a few big breaths, and said adamantly, "No." He didn't think he could handle it. Once again, I was determined to go through labor without drugs. I felt more prepared this time, and my body seemed more relaxed. My hair and makeup in place, I instinctively fell into a breathing rhythm that helped the process along.

Three hours later (my labor was short, only four and a half hours), with my face puffy, red, and covered with sweat, my hair stuck to my forehead and wrapped around my head like a turban, my hands in a deathlike grip on the sides of the bed, I screamed at Steve, "The baby is coming! Get somebody in here to deliver this baby! I don't care who it is! The janitor can do it! Just get someone in here, or I'll jump out the window!" Steve ran out the door, and the next thing I remember is being rolled into the delivery room. What a relief it was not to be tied down to the delivery table! The room was less chaotic, and William entered his new world (they had to induce labor as he was one month past the due date) without shedding a tear. At first his silence frightened me, and I started to panic. "Why isn't he crying?" I nervously asked the doctor. He said calmly with a smile, "He's tired. He was working hard, too." That I understood.

As I was unencumbered by wrist restraints, I leaned up on my elbows to get a peek at my new friend. Just as I did, he looked straight at me. Our eyes locked on each other with an unspoken understanding: we knew we were about to embark on an adventure together. I was excited and blissful. William looked around cautiously and then returned his eyes to my gaze. It was clear he was ready to share his life with me. My little William was everything I was hoping for. He had beautiful blue eyes and a peaches-and-cream complexion. Although he let me know with a thunderous roar when he needed attention, he was easy to care for. He was very inquisitive, and as long as he had new things to examine and explore, he was happy. He'd crawl after me while I cleaned the house, often sitting on the vacuum cleaner as I dragged him from room to room. I cherished our time together. All I'd have to do is say, "Hi, William," and his whole head would beam a smile back at me. He was, and is, delightful. Afraid of nothing and still very curious.

It was 1968. I lived in San Francisco, the birthplace of the Haight-

Ashbury free-love culture. Promiscuity and drugs were the norm. At the time, the worst thing anyone could be called was a hypocrite. The Civil Rights Movement was going strong, and college students, along with many middle-class adults, were protesting the Vietnam War. Martin Luther King was assassinated. Bobby Kennedy was assassinated. Everything was in turmoil. All rules and mores were challenged and, more often than not, discarded. I lived about twenty minutes away from the epicenter and was very intrigued but not ready to go far beyond my doorstep. When the Civil Rights Act was passed in 1968, I was twenty years old and the mother of two children. The Black Power Movement was going full throttle. The front page of the *San Francisco Chronicle* had pictures of the Black Panthers walking down Market Street with rifles hanging from their shoulders. They looked tough, angry, and proud. They scared me. Then came the riots after Martin Luther King Jr. was murdered, resulting in a huge division between the whites and the blacks. I just wanted to fade into the background.

One afternoon, when William was almost two and Joey five, a girlfriend told me someone had seen a woman in Steve's car and it wasn't me. I dismissed it as gossip until during one of our numerous fights, Steve confessed to me that he had a baby with a girl from the local bar. The baby was a girl and about eighteen months older than William. I thought back to the time Steve came to see me in the hospital after I gave birth to William. He came in all dressed up, smelling of cologne, and in a hurry to leave and join his friends at the bar. He was going to see her. Why didn't I realize something was up? I knew he was flirtatious and the girls all loved him, but I just couldn't believe he would betray me. I decided after Steve's betrayal that I no longer wanted to be his wife. When the sad faces I drew on my calendar began to significantly outnumber the happy ones, I knew it was over.

My fights with Steve began to escalate as he could feel he was losing me and he began to freak. Our last fight told both of us things were getting out of hand. He had wrestled me to the floor and was holding me down by the throat. He picked a large ceramic vase off the table beside our bed, raised it over his shoulder, and was about to bring it down across my face. He stopped about two inches above my forehead. I still remember the look in his eyes— intense anger that changed to fear. *What are we doing?* we silently asked each other. He said not a word, put the vase down, and walked out the door. I went to the kitchen, collected all the bottles I had been saving, took them to the store for a refund, got enough money for bus fare, grabbed the boys, and never looked back. I left my Donna Reed role behind and walked out the door at twenty-one, with two kids and little education. I knew my only chance for a better life was to return to school. I reasoned that a minimum-wage job that took me away from my kids full-time was not an option. I took the bus to the local community college and enrolled. I took a step into the unknown, and for the first time in many years, I could finally breathe easier.

I supported myself with the help of welfare and found a babysitter for my two boys. I used to walk about ten blocks to drop the kids off (I had neither a driver's license nor a car), and because they couldn't walk very fast, I put them in a little red wagon, tied a belt around the handle to extend its length, and hurried off down the hill, pulling them behind. When they started school, I arranged my classes to fit my boys' schedule. Later, when welfare cut their day-care funding, I took William with me to college and put him in the day-care center or took him to class with me while Joey was in the first grade. Because we were so broke, I used to hitchhike to and from school, sometimes with the boys. I truly believed (and still do) that I had a protector who would make sure nothing bad would happen to us. That was a fine philosophy for me, but my poor boys, especially Joey, who needed structure and routine, must have often worried and been afraid.

After a couple months of searching, I finally found an apartment that would take a single, unemployed mother of two who was going to school. It was a nice apartment, but unfortunately, it was on the fringes of a rough part of Oakland. If I turned left when leaving the apartment, I found myself in an upper middle-class area. The houses all had nice lawns, the streets were clean, and there was a great ice-cream parlor nearby. I'd scrape some money together, and the boys and I would trot off to get an ice cream, while enjoying ourselves in the nicer neighborhood. If I turned right, I found myself on the edge of a ghetto, with unemployment, poverty, boarded-up buildings, and crime. I was definitely living on the edge and did my best to keep it from my boys.

I was resolute about not raising my children the way my mother raised me. I thought if I kept the house in order and the boys clean, had dinner for them every night, and was involved with their school, everything would be fine. To some extent, that was true. I thought that if things were going bad, they would let me know by acting out or by messing up at school. They never did. They were good boys (and have grown into good men). What I didn't consider was the impact living a free-spirited hippie lifestyle had on them. I was young, learning what it meant to be a young adult in an environment going through intense social change, with no role models or rules to live by. I went to concerts, had parties, smoked dope, and had sex when I felt like it. I tried to shelter the boys from my wild ways and only entertained men when they were asleep. Men did not spend the night unless there was a chance for a relationship. That certainly didn't happen very often. A woman with two kids? No way! They were out of there!

Living in a predominantly African American area meant that I had the opportunity to meet, and date, many young black men. I would meet them on the street, in the grocery store, at school, or in clubs. I loved the funky music that was coming out of the black community and found myself drawn to, what I perceived to be, the exotic world of the black man. And no one (especially my ex-husband, who came from a family of bigots) could tell me I was wrong. By the time I got to college, the Black Power Movement had mellowed somewhat. The black community still demonstrated a tremendous sense of pride, but they seemed less angry. That is, until it came to a white woman dating a black man. More than once when I was walking with a black man, a black woman would glare at me and chastise him. "What are you doing with that white girl? Don't you have any respect for who you are?" Naively, I thought there would be no difference when dating a man from a different culture. After all, my hippie philosophy told me we were all one. I found I could handle insults thrown at me from the white community, but when black women began to confront me, I fell silent and felt guilty. I empathized with their plight as women and began to wonder if it was possible for people from different races to get together and date.

I soon began to understand that America itself was racist and everyone was affected. The black men I dated had their own agenda, as did I. In the 1970s, interracial dating was complicated and rarely genuine. More often than not, one person, or both, was playing some sort of clandestine manipulation of the system and of each other. Today's young people have a healthier understanding of prejudice, and although it has not been eliminated entirely, I am happy to see that bigotry seems to be on the wane.

When I was getting ready to graduate from college, I was determined to take further control of my life. My first step was to get off welfare. With no job and limited possibilities, I met with my welfare worker and told her I wanted to be taken off the welfare rolls. She tried to talk me out of it, but I assured her that I would make it somehow. I had taken EST (a popular consciousness-raising course), which reaffirmed my belief that I was responsible for my own reality. Therefore, I could create my world as I saw fit. I found a part-time job so I could finish school and still bring in some money, but I needed more help from Steve. He had been giving us $50 per month, and that clearly was not enough. Steve was driving a Cadillac while I was hitchhiking to save money. The court awarded me the amount he owed me from the past and increased his child support. I didn't take the money he owed me from the past. What was done was done. I did, however, take the monthly increase from $150 to $325, and I didn't feel guilty about it one bit. When he'd call me irate about this or that, I finally had the nerve to say calmly, "Talk to my lawyer." He began to leave me alone.

I was almost finished with school (it took me seven years to get my four-year degree) and was now taking my classes in the afternoon so I could work in the mornings and evenings. I made it home to check in with the kids, prepare dinner, and grab a bus to make it back to work. Joey was in the eighth grade and was responsible for watching his brother. I left work at 9:00 p.m., dashed to the bus, and ran the last three blocks to be home by 9:30. My stomach was always in knots. I was in a constant state of anxiety, whether in school, at work, or racing the clock to get home before I was officially labeled a "bad mother." I tried to ignore the guilt feelings that kept me awake and did my best to keep my emotions from getting the best of me. I used to have images of my insides spewing out, coating the walls blood-red. Exhausted, I knew I had to keep it together and, once again, compartmentalized my feelings. That helped me make it through the night, but when my children became young adults and our relationship was not as close as I had hoped it would be, all the old feelings of guilt and blame resurfaced. I spent much of my time hurting and beating myself up for not being a better parent.

One night, as I was running up the block to get home from work, I saw two boys playing in the darkness. One was in a shopping cart and was being pushed by another, somewhat older boy. I shook my head, disgusted. What were those young boys doing out like this after dark? What kind of parents let their children play outside this late? As I came closer, I started to see the outline of their faces, laughing and having fun. Oh, no! Those were my boys! Uh-oh. I needed to rethink what was going on. I started to doubt my ability to give them the structure and security they needed, especially as they were about to become teenagers. I began to think about having the boys move in with their father. Steve could offer the boys things I could not. He could offer money, a stay-at-home mom (his wife, Carly, was a wonderful, kind woman who had always been good to my boys), a car, a house, and the stability that came with having two parents. Also, I thought it was a good time for the boys to learn about their father, beyond just weekend baseball games. Joey was about to start high school, and William was about to start the sixth grade. They had been with me during their formative years, and I prayed the things I taught them would not be forgotten. I called Steve for a conference.

Steve was finally ready for the responsibility of taking care of the boys full-time. They were older now and did not need the constant monitoring younger children required. Steve and I both knew Carly would be the one to do the majority of the caretaking, and Steve assured me that she was willing and open to sharing her life, full-time, with the boys. After the decision was made and we agreed about visits and finances, I fell apart. I remember laying my head in Steve's lap, sobbing. I asked him to please not turn my children against me. He said, "What kind of monster do you think I am?" I took him at his word. Big mistake! Not that I could have done anything to prevent his poisonous attacks on me. As his anger toward me continued, I have no doubt that he took out his hatred for me by berating me in front of the boys. To this day, my relationship with the boys continues to be tentative and scarred.

After the boys moved out, I went into their room and cried myself to sleep on their floor. When I awoke, feeling totally depleted and empty, I began to panic. I called my friend Shannon, who had known me for years and had a special fondness for my children. I explained the boys were gone, and I couldn't be alone. I had never been alone, without children, since I was seven years old. My boys were not only my children, they were an integral part of me and who I was. I felt as if someone had ripped a part of my body away, and I was standing there with a gaping hole, gushing blood. I was nauseous, dizzy, and terrified. Had I made the right decision? Would they interpret my action as abandonment and hate me? Would they remember how much I loved them and how I truly did my best to care for them and help them develop values and ethics that would guide them on their path to adulthood? Mainly I prayed that the love I held for them, my two beautiful sons, would be a source of reassurance as they struggled, as we all do, to find their own sense of self-worth.

I wanted to make sure that the boys were settled before I made any drastic changes in my living situation. I put my things (which didn't amount to much) in storage and rented a room from a woman I worked with. Not long after, my job suddenly ended, and I found myself without my children, without a job, and without a place to live. I was down to the bare bones of existence. I started to spiral into a deep depression and began to drink too much. I felt like Dorothy, who, when swept away by the cyclone, helplessly watched all the pieces of her life swirl by. Although I was still Joey and William's mother, my life no longer centered around taking care of them. I felt worthless. I had nothing. I felt like nothing. I was nothing. And I cried—a lot. Eventually my boys adjusted to life with their father. Joey was generally too busy to spend time with his dear old mother, but William spent most weekends with me. After living in a rented room for one year, I found a studio apartment near Ghirardelli Square. I stayed in that apartment for two years, still monitoring the boys' adjustment from a distance. Everything seemed to be going okay.

As I did not have to run home to take care of the boys, I began to focus on my career. I had a college degree but didn't know if I had any marketable skills. I put a resume together and sent a few to local proprietary schools and one to a school in Ventura, California. I remembered the beautiful beaches in Ventura from surfing movies Steve and I used to watch when we were in high school. Much to my surprise, I received several good offers, and the job in Ventura offered me the best salary and benefits. Off I went to reinvent myself in Ventura, staying in contact with the boys by weekly phone calls and monthly visits to the Bay Area. No one knew me in Ventura. I was not Steve's ex-wife, nor Joey and William's mother. I was just me: Linda Lake. I knew it was up to me to either sink or swim. I was determined to succeed and knew, intellectually at least, that I was capable of rising to the top. However, in the middle of the night, I'd often awake, sweating profusely, worried about being discovered for a fraud. Sooner or later, everyone was going to see through my façade, and, like the Wizard of Oz, I'd be exposed as a person who was bluffing. Although my performance met, and even surpassed, the expectations assigned to me by my boss, I had to constantly fight off the demons of doubt. I pushed myself even further, produced more, and became very good at anticipating my boss's needs. It worked. I found I was creative, smart, and did know what I was talking about! Everywhere I looked, I saw new strategies and solutions. I saw only opportunities, not limitations. As a result, nothing was unachievable. I continued to excel at my job and began to acquire more and more responsibilities. I loved what I was doing.

My boys stayed with me every summer, and after they graduated from high school, they moved in with me to attend the computer school where I worked. William was eighteen, and Joey was twenty-one. They hadn't lived with me for five years, and I was not quite prepared for the machismo that had become part of their persona. Yikes! Who raised these macho dudes? I believe they came to Ventura expecting to find their mom partying like crazy. Undoubtedly that was the reason their father gave them for me moving. It was an adjustment for all of us. In order to keep up with the demands of my job, I had to be in bed early and needed the house to be relatively quiet so I could sleep. I discovered that the methods I used for keeping them in line as children no longer worked. They were young men, and I had to find a new approach. Being a single mom, I had no one to confer with on how to handle the situation, and we had quite a few heated arguments.

After a few months, we found a way to live together and settled into a routine. Respect for each other helped us through the transition. After about a year and a half, long enough for them to graduate from computer school, things began to change. My job was being phased out, and it was time for me to move on. I always knew my move to Ventura was temporary. Both of the boys also expressed a desire to eventually move back to San Francisco. I started to plan my return to the Bay Area. The boys left after I did, found jobs back in Northern California, and got on with their lives. I moved in with an old friend, Gary, and found a new job. Shortly after Gary and I moved in together, we discovered we were falling in love. When Gary asked me to marry him, I cried and said "yes." We had a simple ceremony, and I was pleased that at age forty, I was finally in a mature relationship with a man I could trust. And we were having fun!

In the beginning, I didn't think anything of it when Gary would come home every night and fall right asleep. I knew he worked very hard and just thought he was tired. I ignored the fact that when he walked in the front door after work, he went straight to the refrigerator, grabbed a six pack, and slammed down six beers. After a few months, it finally dawned on me. He wasn't falling asleep. He was passing out! I looked the other way. After about five years, I knew we were drifting apart. I wasn't paying much attention to my marriage and was still in denial about Gary's drinking. Planning for our future, I began to look for a way to contribute more to our marriage financially. I decided to go back to school to become a family therapist and applied to graduate school and was accepted. I was thrilled and enthusiastic.

Running on adrenalin, I worked full-time while carrying a full load in the evenings at graduate school. All the while, I was still the top performer at work and graduated with a 4.0 GPA. After finishing my last final, I was driving down the hill from school, enjoying the gorgeous sunset. I looked over, and all of a sudden, my grandfather was in the car with me! His head was floating just above the dashboard! I could smell the Brylcreem he used to wear and started to giggle. I guessed he wanted to celebrate my success and congratulate me on finishing school. I thought it was a bit odd, but it didn't worry me. In fact, I felt oddly at peace and a bit giddy. When I later told my sister about the visit, she insisted I was hallucinating, probably from exhaustion. I knew better. Dada had come to be with me, only I wasn't sure why.

A few days later, I awoke in the middle of the night to go to the bathroom and discovered I was urinating blood. I woke Gary up, and we went to the emergency room. I had my incomplete thesis under my arm, convinced that I could use my time in the hospital to work on my dissertation. The nurse that admitted me took one look at me and the books I was carrying and shook her head and said, "Type A personality, eh?" I ignored her sarcastic remark. They weren't sure what was wrong with me and began to run tests. I still thought it was something minor until the pain started. Wow! Work on my thesis? Forget it! This hurts! I was told I was passing a kidney stone and waited for it to pass. Passing a kidney stone hurts as much as having a baby, except nothing good comes out of it at the end. And this "kidney stone" wasn't budging.

An oncologist stopped by the next morning and told me I had cancer of the kidney. He explained that if the cancer was in my lymph nodes (which they wouldn't know until they operated), my chance for a full recovery went down to 20 percent. Gulp. Hold on, lymph nodes! Don't let that sucker in! I then realized why Dada had come to me! To let me know he was with me as I fought the cancer demon. After a brief pity party, I turned my thoughts to life and survival. I was not going out without a fight. I began to filter out any negative forces and/or thoughts and look for ways to enhance my chances of survival. My surgeon explained I would probably need five units of blood, and as the blood bank might be carrying tainted blood, suggested I ask my family for blood donations. That would take time, however, at least a couple of weeks. I said, "No. I want that cancer out of me *now*." I would take my chances. The operation was scheduled, and I began to prepare for the toughest battle I was yet to face.

I called three of my dearest friends: Maria, Shannon, and Carly. I had known them for years and knew they truly cared about me and were incredibly insightful women who saw and understood things beyond the obvious. I needed them with me as I reached out to the angels I saw out of the corner of my eye who were floating above my shoulder.

I tapped into my friends' power and used their energy to help me heal. We held a ritual in my room to scour the cancer from my body. We chanted, prayed, and even lit sage for a brief second. I had my mother bring me a tape with positive, subliminal messages to listen to while I was in surgery. After working my way through the bureaucracy, the hospital administrators finally said I could wear headphones and listen to my tape in the operating room. Once everything was in place, I went deep into my soul and became very quiet. As I was being wheeled into the operating room, I slowed my breathing down and put myself in a trance. I was not worried or agitated at all. I was very calm. The universe embraced me and held me in its arms. I felt as if I was in a cocoon, protected and loved.

When I awoke, the doctor told me he believed he had gotten all of the tumor and it had not spread to the lymph nodes. Now, it was just a matter of making it past two years, then five. After that, the odds of a reoccurrence diminished significantly. As the doctor was leaving, he turned to me and said in disbelief, "I don't know how you did it, but you didn't lose any blood. You didn't need any transfusions. I've never had that happen before." I smiled and looked up at Dada. Thank you, I whispered and slowly closed my eyes.

Several things changed after I faced the possibility of dying. My first response was to begin writing a list of all the things I needed to do before I died. As my life's timeline had been extended, the list was no longer important. My intention became to live every single day to its fullest. So much of my life had been about planning and thinking ahead; I now realized I had missed the extraordinary moments in between. I was determined not to miss any more of those "in between" moments. I began to appreciate my friends and family with a newfound appreciation. I worked hard at letting go of past irritants and began to loosen up and let people and things just be. I purposely slowed my gait and made a concerted effort to relax my shoulders and pay attention to what messages the universe was sending me.

A year after my cancer diagnosis, Gary decided he didn't want to be married anymore. I thought the fact that we were friends many years before we became lovers meant we would stay together and work out any problems that arose. I was wrong. Once again, my reoccurring abandonment issues surfaced. After three months of mourning the end of my marriage, I bought some new clothes that flattered my thinner body (I had lost a tremendous amount of weight), got a new, spiky haircut, stopped coloring the gray streak in my hair, and found a job that paid me significantly more money than I had ever made before. I was on my way, more conscious, clear, and "on purpose."

Not long after my separation from Gary, I knew I was ready for another relationship. I was through repeating stale and unresolved issues within the context of old patterns and negative associations. I wanted a partner to share my life with, not to complete me but to add to what I had become: a strong, accomplished woman worthy of love and happiness.

Three months after Gary and I split up, I wrote a very specific list of what I wanted in a man and called in two of my dear friends, Maria and Joe. We held a very detailed ritual to banish jealousy, insecurity, envy, self-doubt, and so on, and to create abundance, love, peace, safety, confidence, and a *good man*! Three weeks later, I met my good man, Allen, and right away, both of us knew something special was going on. He is strong, interesting, funny, and gorgeous. Although a strong man, with definite opinions, he is willing to listen and learn. I love him dearly. We have been together for over fifteen years and still thank our lucky stars we found each other.

As Allen and I were learning about each other and how to love with an open heart, I got the news that my mother had stage IV lung cancer. She had been a heavy smoker for years and had quit ten years earlier, but the damage was done. I was the happiest I had ever been and wanted to share this extraordinary time with my mom. Unfortunately there was little time left. My poor mother was dying. I thought about all the time I wasted being angry with her and shutting her out. The doctor gave her only a couple of weeks to live, and although very remorseful and ashamed, I tried my best to spend my limited time with her by being present with no agendas.

Mom decided against chemotherapy because it made her so sick. Additionally, as the cancer was so advanced, it really wasn't going to extend her life to any degree. She decided to do her best to fight the pain with morphine. She wanted to stay alert and be with us as long as she could. One afternoon, she and I stood together, looking out the window at the bare trees and gray skies, not saying a word. Nothing was moving, not even the dead leaves on the patio floor. It was as if everything had stopped, allowing us to be together. It was only us. After a few minutes of just standing close, I asked her if she was afraid. She said, "No." In fact, she said that since it was going to happen, she was glad it was in the winter. It would have been harder for her to leave with the sun shining and children playing outside. We continued to stand there, looking straight ahead. We couldn't bring ourselves to look into each other's eyes. There was too much to say and not enough time to say it. We couldn't bear to see the hurt and regret in each other's eyes.

After she became so sick and was in terrible pain, I'd climb into her bed, put my arms around her, and try to massage the pain from her back. During those times, we were very close. No pretenses, no inhibitions, no baggage from the past. We were just sharing an intimate moment as mother and daughter. That is one of the lessons I want to pass on to my children: life is short. Please don't waste time being angry or leave things unsaid. It's bad for the spirit and the body.

Mom died December 26. Toward the end, she'd sleep most of the time, and we tried to keep her pain under control with the help of morphine and the hospice nurse. Christmas was always a very important time for our family. We'd all get together on Christmas Eve and prepare a hectic meal, some peeling potatoes in the kitchen, some frantically tearing lettuce leaves apart to make an almost-forgotten salad. We would often pull biscuits from the oven after the outside was burned ("but the insides are still good!" someone would say reassuringly) and start dinner with not everything ready at the same time. But we were all at the table, together, laughing and telling stories. We all loved Christmas. Especially my Mom.

On her last Christmas Eve, I went and bought us a Christmas dinner from the local supermarket and with paper plates and napkins, tried to set up a table in a spare apartment in my mother's building. Everyone nibbled a bit, saying they weren't hungry, and went back to my mother's apartment. Suddenly we heard a commotion from upstairs and nervously looked at one another, not knowing what to expect. There, at the top of the stairs, stood my mother. Her head bald, her belly swollen, an old robe wrapped around her, and with a twinkle in her eye, she yelled down to us, "I want turkey and cranberry sauce!" Holding onto the stair rail, she eased herself down and made it to the chair. Someone scrambled to fix her a plate (which she never ate, of course). She wanted to spend Christmas with us. She didn't want our future Christmases to be clouded with memories of her final days.

When it became evident that the end was near, we called the hospice nurse. Mom was in so much pain she couldn't talk. All of my sisters were in the kitchen not far from where my mother and I were sitting, arguing with the nurse. The noise level was rising, and suddenly my mother turned to me and pleaded with her eyes to have the girls quiet down. I knew she was not happy about them talking about her as if she wasn't in the room. I turned to my sisters and the nurse and asked them to lower their voices and to talk to my mother directly if they had something to say that concerned her. They quieted down, walked over to my mom, and talked to her about what was happening. After the nurse left, I whispered to my mom, "Dose yourself, Mom. We can take care of ourselves." She looked deeply into my eyes, and I knew she had given herself permission to leave. She died the next morning, the day after Christmas. She made it through Christmas for us.

I received the call in the middle of the night. She had passed, but I was invited to come and see her. I drove right over and went straight to her room. She looked so pretty! Her skin was flawless, and she still had those classic features that formed her beautiful face. She looked peaceful. Her little pink tongue was protruding from her mouth just barely. She looked like a beautiful baby resting quietly. I sat with her awhile, told her she still looked pretty, thanked her for trying so hard, and reminded her that we were all adults and could take care of ourselves. She didn't have to worry anymore. The funeral home was called, and my sisters went to the spare apartment while her body was removed. They said they couldn't handle seeing her taken away under a sheet. I, on the other hand, knew the body being carried down the stairs was not my mother. It was only her vessel. She had already been released from the physical pain she had suffered with her illness and from the emotional pain she lived with from trying to please everyone and not knowing how. Finally she was free.

A few months after my mother's death, my sister Eileen whispered to me, "I don't have to be the good one anymore." I was a bit perplexed by her statement, and its significance failed to register with me. By this time, Eileen was thirty-eight years old, with a failed marriage and fed up with the job she had had for several years. With little effort, she found another job and was ready to embark on a new career with fresh opportunities and more money. I know she was scared. Was she really capable of being successful? Did she really deserve happiness? After her last day at her old job, where she was ushered out the door with barely a "thank you" for all of her years of service, she headed to the bar and got very drunk. She was, I am sure, crushed about her insignificant send-off.

After she left the bar, while driving in one of California's worst rainstorms, she skidded off the side of the road, totaling her car. She was picked up by the police and arrested for driving under the influence. Eileen was released from jail early Saturday morning. She took a cab to an ATM, withdrew enough money to cover her transportation home, went to her condo, stripped the bed, put on one of my mother's old T-shirts, and curled up in a blanket.

When Eileen did not show up at her new job on Monday morning, they called Elizabeth, who, with Stephanie, went to investigate. Driving up to Eileen's condo, all seemed quiet, almost too quiet. Nothing was unusual except that her car was not in the driveway. Elizabeth had a key to Eileen's condo, and together they slowly opened the front door. They were immediately struck by a horrific odor, the likes of which they had never before experienced. They tiptoed in, calling Eileen's name out softly, and inched their way back to Eileen's bedroom. Peering around the corner, their eyes slowly adjusting to the early morning light, they saw a large mound wrapped in a blanket on the unmade bed. Trembling and fighting intense nausea, they moved forward until they could go no further and froze. The only thing recognizable was a patch of auburn hair peeking out of the top of the blanket. Thankfully, most of Eileen's cold, motionless, bloated, and purple body was out of view. Both my sisters began to howl and run in and out of the condo. They were traumatized with what they had found and didn't know what to do. Their beloved sister, Eileen, was dead, and they were not sure why or how it happened.

She must have been contemplating suicide for quite a while, because she had been stockpiling my mother's morphine. When it was time, Eileen made sure to take the drug slowly, so she wouldn't throw it up before it did its job. Before long, she was asleep, never to wake and face the sorrow she had lived with for most of her life. There was a note later found by the police that simply stated, "I'm sorry." Her statements like "I don't have to be the good one anymore," her increased alcohol consumption, and the sly look on her face, as if she held a big secret, were just a few of the signs that had clearly said, "Help me." None of us noticed. She was thirty-eight years old.

When I got home from work that evening, I found a message from my brother-in-law on my machine. I was to call my sister's house, immediately. I called, knowing from the tone of his voice that something was terribly wrong. He answered the phone, and upon hearing my voice, simply cried out, "Eileen's dead!" I fell to the floor and began to scream. I couldn't imagine Eileen was dead and then discovered she had killed herself. I couldn't imagine our family without her. She was too important to us. She had decided to die, and my whole family was devastated and I was enraged. I couldn't get rid of the screaming inside my head and found myself shaking uncontrollably.

I had nightmares for months and couldn't shake the guilt. I should have recognized the signs of her impending suicide. I should have been able to rescue her. If only I had noticed. If only I had been paying more attention. I felt her decision to end her life was incredibly selfish and stupid. It took me many years to forgive her and forgive myself for not stepping in and rescuing my little sister. When I finally was able to forgive, the black hole in my heart began to heal, and I discovered a newfound love for her and for myself. My memories of our time together became more enjoyable, and I no longer dwelled on the "What if?" that had plagued me for years, telling me I could have stopped her if only I hadn't been so insensitive.

Allen, the man who came to me after Maria, Joe, and I created the model for my good man, became my rock during this dreadful time. He brought my wish list to life. I had asked for a partner who loved to travel, was well educated, and was successful, adventurous, childlike, and strong. While I was healing, he'd often just hold me, my emotions wildly erupting, and rarely say a word. When I was ready, he held out his hand and began to show me that life could still be glorious.

Allen has been to over 185 countries and continues to explore unusual, remote places. When we were married by the village Shaman on the Belize River, he promised to show me the world. He has certainly lived up to his promise. We have traveled the globe together, and I have seen things I had only read about in books.

A woman in Cairo invited me into her hovel. We sat together on a dirt floor and looked up beyond the crumbling walls to the sky. She proudly presented me with a loaf of bread straight from her stone oven. Although we did not speak each other's language, when our eyes met, I saw a common experience: she was a mother, providing for her family, creating normalcy in the midst of dust and smoke. Women are incredibly resourceful. With a glint in her eye, she was surviving.

In the Amazon, two young girls giggled with me and blushed when they walked into my room and found me and my husband loving each other in bed. They came to clean our room, working hard in the midmorning sun in order to earn money to send their children to school. Women are hard workers. Finding time to capture a loving moment with their laughter, they were surviving.

In the Middle East, amid rubble behind a twenty-foot-tall cement barricade, a weary mother with grit in her hair took the time to offer me a cup of tea. In the midst of a war, facing challenges every day that I cannot begin to fathom, children playing at her feet, she still was willing to open her heart. Women are resilient. In the midst of war, while sharing some tea with a stranger, she was surviving.

In Asia, a modest woman quietly walked by with her baby strapped to her chest. She stopped to look at the wares being offered in the marketplace, and I found myself drawn to her child. She noticed my interest and stopped. With a smile that lit up the darkness, she proudly showed me her baby. She took such delight in the fact that I, too, could love her child! We spoke not a word as we shared a universal love for children. She went on her way with her body covered in what we Westerners would consider rags, and continued her shopping. Stepping gently around the cattle dung and muddy waters, she was on her way home to take care of her family. With strength and fortitude, she was surviving.

In Benin, Africa, I stood and watched in awe as a group of women sat in a circle, singing and playing drums. I couldn't help but move my body to the tempo they provided. In the center of the circle was a woman who appeared to be the oldest. Her eyes caught mine, and we smiled. She then gestured to her friends, who slowly opened the circle near where I was standing and motioned for me to join them. I moved ahead, the circle closed around me, and suddenly my body began to dance in an unfamiliar/familiar way. The lady elder removed her scarf and wrapped it gently around my neck. We moved together, feeling the earth's rhythm. In time, the circle reopened, she removed her scarf from my neck, and I exited the circle, dancing, our eyes still focused on each other. With optimism and joy, in the midst of poverty, violence, chaos, and uncertainty, she was surviving.

Each excursion I have taken with Allen has reaffirmed some basic truths. No matter what one's culture, economic status, religion, or race, we all strive for the same things: shelter, a world free from war, good food, health care, an education for our children, and clean air and water. That certainly is not too much to ask for.

I have now been cancer free for fifteen years. I no longer panic if I feel strange, or if I see a bruise that I can't explain. Don't get me wrong; I still pay attention, but it no longer runs my life. My two boys are now grown with families of their own. I am very proud of them. They are good men and wonderful fathers to my three grandchildren. Watching them as fathers, husbands, and sons, I realize that I must have been a good mother after all! It is time to let go of the guilt! For years, I held the mistaken belief that I did not deserve a good life. I was trapped in a drama of shame. That belief is no longer appropriate. As Maya Angelou says, "I did what I thought was right with what I knew then. Now that I know more, I can do better." And I do. The shame is finally slipping from my shoulders. I am not perfect, but I am proud of what I have become. My relationships have improved greatly, and I like whom I see when I look in the mirror. I no longer see the ugly Sid Caesar with the mole and big nose. Instead, I see eyes that sparkle, lines that speak of my adventures, and a smile that is not forced.

While writing this story, I came to see that after every crisis—and there were many—I survived. I may have been knocked down from time to time, but I found the determination to stand back up. After every sleepless night, worrying about my children or money, I awoke and eventually found something to smile at. All it took was a kind woman's look in my direction, a phone call from a special friend, or a prayer whispered in the darkness to remind me that "This, too, shall pass." I am so grateful for my soul sisters, who were right there with me, and for my husband, who now stands by my side. Thanks to their reassurance, understanding, and generosity, I am closer to my true self. If I become doubtful or confused, I wrap my arms around my chest and breathe. I know I can handle anything, and I am not afraid.

"From Hand to Hand and Heart to Heart" is an excerpt from a book to be published in its entirety at a later date.

The Building Blocks of Character
"Character cannot be developed in ease and quiet.
Only through experience of trial and suffering can the
soul be strengthened, ambition inspired, and success achieved."
—Helen Keller

10 Inspiring Quotes for a Depressed Heart. Accessed December 22, 2010.
http://www.beliefnet.com/Health/Emotional-Health/Depression/

Introducing Soul Sister Arrenia Corbin

I MET ARRENIA CORBIN WHEN we were both medical assistants in OB-GYN at San Francisco Kaiser Permanente. She arrived after I started my employment in 1967 with Kaiser Permanente. At this time in my life, I was trying desperately to have new starts and beginnings. I was determined to keep my new job and all the benefits it afforded me, such as health care coverage for my young son and myself. It also allowed me to live independently. There were opportunities here for me, but first I had to get out of survival mode and get into caring for myself and my young child.

It was at this time I decided to leave my husband because I rarely saw him. Sometimes three weeks would pass before he came by, and then he would crash at my little apartment for days. He was highly involved in drug use, and this changed him into a controlling and physically abusive person. I began to fear him and have anxiety attacks in his presence. I no longer felt safe with him around my little son because his behavior was unpredictable. I planned an escape from him and went into hiding. I paid a huge price for this action when he found me three weeks later. It is still difficult for me to recall the physical battering I received when he found me. When I recovered enough to get to the police, I filed an assault and battery charge against him. He spent three months in jail for his actions, and he never hit me again from then on. I began a new life without him.

I found work to be a safe and wonderful new place to learn about the health care field. I was thirsty for all the knowledge I was learning, and I enjoyed working with the doctor who selected me to be his assistant. By the time I met Arrenia at work, I was still in the process of changing my personal life for the better.

She arrived in 1968 with the hiring of several other medical assistants, who were the first African Americans in the department. We were all in our early twenties at the time, except for Beatrice, who was older and had already established herself in the department as a housekeeper prior to becoming a medical assistant. I liked Arrenia best of all the new gals because she seemed not to say much but always knew what was going on. She would just have that look about her with a gentle smile.

Since I was friends with everyone, we all shared laughs and stories while we roomed the patients for their doctor's appointment, and while we performed our daily assignments. One day—I really do not remember how it all came about—Arrenia asked me if I would like to come to her house because she had lots of clothes she wanted to give away. I was more than happy to go. I was living on a very limited budget with no extras, and clothes would be considered an extra at that time. Well, the day came, and I went to Arrenia's house. She still lived with her mother; it was before she was engaged to be married to her lifelong love, Donald Corbin.

Her mom was really nice to me and made me feel very welcome as she sat down in a comfortable armchair to join us as we went through the heap of clothes that was on the floor in the living room between us all.

This is how I got my dark red leather trench coat. It was beautiful to me and fit perfectly, with still lots of life in it. I looked real good in it too. Arrenia's mother selected an outfit off the top of the heap of clothes; it was a silky shirt and skirt to match, with pink flowers with a cream color background. As she raised it to her shoulders, she said, "Well, this is a pretty frock!" I thought to myself, What's *a "frock"*? I then immediately dismissed it, thinking it must mean an outfit.

In any event, I left her house that day with a spring in my step, feeling like a queen with my new wardrobe compliments of my coworker and friend Arrenia. To be part of the working poor and to have someone come out of the blue and just ask me if I would like some clothes was wonderful to me. It brought a little bit of sunshine into my life. Arrenia cared enough about me to offer me some clothes that were in perfect shape with lots of life left; it made me feel so very special. I now had a new outfit for the Christmas party at work. It was a beautiful lavender velvet dress, with lace at the base of the long sleeves. I loved it.

Unless you are living with little to nothing, I do not think you can realize the full impact someone from work, whom you do not know on a personal level, thinking about helping you by providing beautiful clothes has. No one can quite understand the gratitude one feels with this most generous act of kindness.

As the years passed, I remarried. I was still very much in love with my ex-husband but knew we could never be together again because I was not safe in his presence. I met my second husband, Phillip, who was Irish, at a party, and he seemed nice. He was good-looking, pleasant, and at times very funny.

The most important trait he had was being very kind and good to my little son. After four months, he wanted to get married and pushed hard for it. I knew I was not marrying him for the right reasons. At this time in my life, I did not think I could ever truly love again. However, being married would afford me a better lifestyle for myself and my son, and in my young mind, it was not a bad trade-off. I wanted to get married before having any more children. This was one thing I was certain of, and in order to have another child, I knew getting married would have to be a part of it. This was my best plan at the time to start a new life.

I was delighted that shortly after we were married, I became pregnant. I had waited a long time to do it right, but this baby was not meant to be in my life for a long time. I was about six months pregnant when I was leaking the amniotic fluid and was in terrible, burning pain. It was the Christmas season, and we were celebrating in Burlingame, California, with my in-laws when the inevitable happened. After the family gathering, my husband went out to join some friends because Burlingame was his hometown and in his opinion, this meant a party with his buddies at a local tavern. The pain became so unbearable that I went out to search for him so he could take me to the hospital. I found him drunk with his buddies, standing outside of the tavern in town. It took a while for him to understand what was happening to me, but he was too drunk to drive. We went back to his aunt's house, where I gave him lots of coffee to help sober him up. He managed to drive me into San Francisco so I could go to the emergency department there.

Unfortunately, I was having a spontaneous abortion, or in other words, a miscarriage. Since I was only six months along, they could not save my baby. I could not believe what was happening to me after planning this pregnancy. At that time, you went through the procedure of losing your baby without any emotional support. After eight hours of labor, I delivered my dead baby boy. The pathology report stated he was normal. It was heartbreaking, and I was crushed emotionally not only for the loss of my baby but because his father was not sober enough to be there for me when I needed him the most. These were the turning points in my marriage that I realized could not be repaired or forgiven. It was 1969, a time when no one named their babies when they lost them. If they were stillborn, there were no legal documents or death certificates or memorial services. You just went home with an empty heart and arms. I named my baby boy Patrick Ryan.

But God is good, and in the next few months, I was pregnant again and delivered a beautiful baby boy the following year. He was not born healthy, and there were multiple problems, such as two holes in his heart and a deformity of round shoulders. When he was five, he underwent major surgery to correct his deformity, and after years of follow-up and another surgery, he was on his way to recovery. All this time, I worked in San Francisco and his surgeries were scheduled there as well, so all I had to do was go across the street from the clinic to the hospital to be with him. I spent two months caring for him while he was in the hospital, going home only to sleep at night.

I had been married a few years when Arrenia was engaged to Donald, and soon her wedding was coming. We were all excited as we accepted her wedding invitation to attend her reception and after-party. The day soon came, and there were something like seven hundred guests at her after-party. I remember being one of four people there who were not African American. I did not feel out of place or uncomfortable because everyone was celebrating, partying, and dancing the night away. It was the first time in my young adult life of being so outnumbered by another culture and race. I only knew the bride and groom, and yet I felt very accepted and comfortable as their guests.

My only disappointment at Arrenia and Donald's wedding was that my husband drank way too much; he was the only one who needed help out to the car because of his drunkenness. I was embarrassed, hurt, and heartbroken, but I tried to hide my feelings while there at the party. This marriage did not pass the test of time because of his drinking. Alcoholism played a major role in the demise of his job and our marriage. We had even relocated from Cotati to Sebastopol for him not to visit his friends because he would drink with them. Nothing seemed to help, and he always found a way to drink, which in turn impacted our household budget. Our marriage of convenience lasted eight years, and in 1977, my second marriage ended in a divorce.

I was soon on my own again, now with two boys. I was terrified to start over again and with even greater responsibilities, but it was at this time in my life that I decided I was worth something too. I realized I had a vote in life and how I lived my life was up to me. I knew it would be an uphill battle, but I was determined to win in this game called life. I began to think real hard about who I wanted to have as a life partner. I was still young at age thirty. I knew there must be someone out there who could love me and treat me right. In 1978, I met the man of my dreams. He was a small businessman in the town of Sebastopol, California, and he lived in the same town as I did. He was really kind to me, and he had a way of sweeping me off my feet.

From 1969 to 1981, I had been commuting to work some 130 miles a day, mainly because I loved my job in San Francisco. However, the time involved in commuting and the expense of gas and toll bridges were becoming way too expensive to continue. I transferred to another facility in Sonoma County with the same employer. My job in San Francisco arranged a farewell party for me. Arrenia came to my farewell party as we all went to the Hungry I restaurant in San Francisco. It meant a lot to me that Arrenia came, because I knew I would miss seeing her every day at our workstation. It was November

1981 when I started a new life for myself in Sonoma County with a new husband. This marriage was no picnic since it had the ups and downs of a blended family. However, we both loved each other very much, and I think that was the deciding factor for both of us.

Throughout these years, Arrenia was like an angel that came to me. I would see her at student leadership conferences when she brought high school students with her to attend the conferences. We would see each other at health care fairs, and we would smile across the room at each other. It took only a glance from each other to know everything was fine with us.

As the years passed, Arrenia and I were promoted into managerial positions. Arrenia was the manager in the outpatient medical records department (OPMRD) at San Francisco Medical Center, which was a huge department with a very large staff. I had just landed a management job in OPMRD in South Sacramento (SSC). Before I was to officially start at SSC, I decided to visit seven OPMRDs throughout the Northern California region. I was really looking forward to visiting my dear friend again when I discovered she was the manager in San Francisco.

It was in the fall of 1992 when I arrived in the morning to see Arrenia in her department. It was one of those days that nothing could go wrong because I was so excited to meet up with her again. There she was in her office with a huge plastic baby bottle on her desk. I was filled with confusion as I asked her about it. She said to me, "Well, I have a lot of employees here, and whenever they want to act like a bunch of babies, I place this baby bottle on the counter out there to let them know what I think." We shared a good laugh together, and it seemed like no time had passed between us. What I did discover was that Arrenia had the very best in teamwork among her employees in spite of her big baby bottle—or maybe that was the key to her success.

In between the student leadership conferences, health fairs, and OPMRD regional meetings, Arrenia was frequently in my life. I will always be eternally grateful for knowing such a special lady. Her grace, gentle quietness, and grounded mannerism have always been a respite for me. So it did not surprise me that when I invited her to join me in writing *Soul Sisters, Come on to My House*, she would join me in this endeavor. She was the first person I knew of a different race than me who invited me to her house and shared the gift of giving. Just like with Linda, through knowing Arrenia, I discovered the value of helping, caring, including, and supporting each other. It was last Christmas that I decided to send Arrenia a special gift, a beautiful black velvet evening gown, to thank her for all her generosity so many years ago.

If we had not taken the time at work to get to know each other, we would never have known how much common ground we shared. Here are just a few of our commonalities:

- We both worked in the same career choice in the medical field as medical assistants, with the same employer for decades, and met each other working in the same department.
- We both became managers of the same departments with the same employer but at different locations.
- Both our mothers had breast cancer. Arrenia continues to be a care provider to her mother. In 1989, my mother died of breast cancer after a three-year battle. I, too, was her care provider for two years during her illness.
- Both our first grandsons were stricken with life-threatening illnesses. Her first grandson was diagnosed with sickle cell disease at an early age. My first grandson was diagnosed with leukemia at the age of seven. We both know the pain and heartache of having a grandchild with such debilitating diseases.
- We both had ectopic pregnancies in our young lives. Arrenia describes her painful experience and how it impacted her life. My ectopic pregnancy was also extremely painful and terrifying when it was misdiagnosed. We both experienced emergency surgeries due to ectopic pregnancies.
- We both were in severe car accidents that changed our lifestyles forever.
- We both have undergone painful and long recovery periods due to our multiple injuries. We have both had multiple surgeries due to these injuries.
- We were both placed in rehab centers (skilled nursing facilities) before our time. It is quite a different story when you are not the age of everyone else and yet you are placed in a home for the elderly before your time. The only thought is … *When do I get out of here?*
- We are both spiritually connected. Arrenia and I both have religion as a mainstay in our lives. For me, it has been the only constant in my life. Prayer for both Arrenia and me is vital in explaining who we are as people and how we choose to live our lives on a daily basis.

On April 15, 2010, I went to Arrenia's office to visit and to hear her life story. While I waited in the lobby, an older African American woman called out my name in a soft and questioning voice, "Susan?" She was sitting right next to me, and I could tell from her voice that she had had a stroke; she was holding a walker to assist her with walking. After she turned her head toward me and said my name, I looked at her very closely, studying her face. The years seemed to melt away, for it was Beatrice Ronald. She was one of the very first medical assistants that I had worked with way back in 1967. Yes, of course, the years had aged both of us, but Beatrice, being older than I by several years, had gone through some trying times. We smiled and laughed at the wonderful discovery of seeing an old friend after so many years had passed.

In her day, Beatrice was very feisty. I would say you did not mess with her because she would put you straight with her attitude; she would walk away so confident and clever. I admired her ability to shrug off others with an attitude, as I at the time was scared and shy of anyone with authority. But here she was today an older lady, quiet and soft-spoken, holding her walker as the therapist called her name for her appointment. Just at the same time, Arrenia came out of her office and called me forward. We each walked together in the same direction, and for one moment in time, we all three shared a special moment of being together again. Once in Arrenia's office, she shared with me that Beatrice had suffered several strokes that left her disabled in functioning and walking. Arrenia also let me know Beatrice was a godmother to one of her children. What a wonderful moment to share with two good friends.

I know of no one who has ever said an unfavorable word about Arrenia. She has been selected as my soul sister for her gift of kindness, love, and support to others who need it. Here is her story.

"GOING THROUGH A JOURNEY"
by Arrenia Corbin

GROWING UP IN SAN FRANCISCO, our house was always known as the "community house." Even though we never had much ourselves, it was not uncommon for someone to ring our doorbell and ask for something to eat. I remember one day having lunch with my brothers and sisters when the doorbell rang. I rushed to the door, and when I opened it, I saw a tall, rugged-looking white man. He looked like he had not showered in many days. He was wearing a long tweed overcoat, hat, and scarf. His hair was shoulder length, and his beard was full and unkempt. He said that someone had told him that he could come to our house to get something to eat. As usual, I yelled down the hallway to my mom, "There's someone at the door who would like something to eat." My mom came to the door and looked at the man. She told him to wait there and she would bring him a sandwich. After a few minutes, he left with a sandwich in his hand, very grateful for something to eat. I went back to the table wondering how we could always feed the world when we had so little to eat ourselves. Later in my life, I realized just how blessed we were. I related our story to the Bible story about the little boy with two fishes and five loaves of bread that fed the multitudes. We were able to feed others because of God's amazing grace.

I thought of that when I was asked to share my story in *Soul Sisters, Come on to My House.* In my house growing up, we practiced feeding our souls by how we treated others who came to our house. We always shared the little bit of food that we had, and somehow we always had enough to feed everyone. We shared the clothes that we had outgrown, and they were always in the best condition.

We practiced feeding and nurturing our soul every time my parents invited another family to stay with us to get back on their feet. Our home was often a refuge for people who needed to get back on their feet. This was a blessing that my parents showed my brothers and sisters and me from a very early age.

Because of the many steel mill and train-yard jobs in Richmond, California, many African Americans migrated from the South to Richmond. My parents were from Greenville, Mississippi, and they moved to Richmond in 1946. After my father got established, they moved from Richmond to San Francisco, which is where I was raised. Back then, there was not a delivery room at my San Francisco hospital, so even though my mom had her prenatal care in San Francisco, they had to drive to Oakland to the delivery room where I was born. We lived in a huge house with an upstairs and a downstairs. I come from a large family, so word spread quickly to other family members that my parents were going to California. After my parents got settled in, other men from the family would move from the South and join them. The man from the family would come and stay with my parents while he got on his feet. Once he became employed, he would send for his wife and children, who would then also migrate to the area. This was a normal practice, and usually a family would live with us until the father was back on his feet.

Because we had so many people staying at our house, my parents would usually buy a hundred pounds of potatoes and fifty pounds of sugar. We made biscuits, sewed clothes together, and did whatever it took to help out the family. This was another part of the migration from the South to the North that many people do not know about, but in which my mother and father played a very large part. They were always involved in helping others make a new life for themselves, and I remember many ways in which my family worked to make life better for everyone around us.

When I was a little girl, I remember quite a few experiences with discrimination. Back then, there was a great deal of housing discrimination, and African Americans were not able to buy homes in certain neighborhoods of San Francisco or stay at exclusive hotels. My godparents were at the forefront in bringing about change for the African American community. For example, my godmother, who was a maid for a very well-known family in San Francisco, would go out to some of the neighborhoods that were known for not allowing African Americans equal access to housing and see if she would be allowed to buy a house. She and her husband would take me as her child from place to place and see who would turn us away without reason. Often we would be turned away without even being given the opportunity to see the house, or we wouldn't be given a contract.

Other times, we picketed around exclusive high-rise hotels where they denied African Americans the right to stay. There was one time when I was a little girl that we were protesting in front of a very high-end hotel. I remember hearing people yell racist comments like, "Niggers, go. Go back to the area where you belong." Then someone spit on me. The men picketing wanted to fight, but the church ministers held them back. It is interesting to note that as an adult, I have gone back to that hotel as a guest of honor. Whenever we faced discrimination, my godmother would report it, and the NAACP and lawyers would look into it. Discrimination didn't end after my childhood.

In 1988, while working, I was asked to visit another site where no one knew me and speak about my work experiences working with a diverse staff and its employee relation issues. I went to the facility where the meeting was located and entered the building. I was wearing a power suit and was carrying a briefcase. When I entered the meeting room, I noticed it was filled with predominantly older white men. One of the first men who saw me approached me to tell me that I was in the wrong room. He told me that the housekeeping meeting was down the hall. I knew that I had the right room, so while he stood there waiting for me to leave, I looked around the room and noticed the snack table. They had coffee, tea, bagels, and Danish rolls for the meeting, so I made my way over to the food and started to help myself. I watched him and waited for him to sit down. After he took his seat, I sat down right next to him, just to prove that I was not intimidated. Shortly after we sat down, the facilitator, who was running the meeting, introduced me. As I made my way to give my presentation, I looked over my shoulder at the man who had directed me to the housekeeping meeting. I let him know in a glance that I knew exactly where I belonged.

Some of my most important beliefs, I learned from my parents. Religion and faith in God are the first two. They are as much a part of my daily life as eating and breathing, but they are also something much greater too. They are a part of my soul. When I think about what the word "soul" means to me, I think it is what is deep down inside of you. For example, soul means to me that deep in your heart, you have a love and ability to reach beyond yourself. Soul means to me your morals and your values and how you feel and how you think. Soul also means that you treasure yourself. It means that you value and treasure yourself. It is how you want to feel about yourself. It's as if you are a good steward and caretaker deep in your soul.

Religion and faith in God mean looking beyond yourself and seeing that you can always reach out and help someone else. They mean appreciating yourself and others and spreading love. They are also about being proud of who you are and knowing that there is no one better than you. In my family, we were taught that while there may always be those who have more than you, it doesn't mean they are better than you. My parents expected us to live by these principles without question, and these are the same principles I've found myself repeating verbatim to my children. I always wanted to give my children a different opportunity and understanding, so at a certain age, I asked my children what these principles meant to them. I wanted to hear what they had to say. I wanted to give them an opportunity to express themselves and see that they understood what these principles are all about.

In talking about religion, I'm brought back to thinking about what feeds my soul, "soul food." Soul food to me is the fellowship of everyone gathering together, and a "soul meal" is really about the fellowship of the meal. It means having all the family and relatives come over for dinner. In a soul meal, everyone contributes. The men hunted for rabbits or brought live chickens.

They would bring them home so we could prepare and cook them. We would have to skin the rabbits or wring the chicken necks in the garage to get them ready to cook. While we worked, we sang gospel songs, especially since my parents would not allow any blues or rock 'n' roll in the house.

The preparation for our soul meal would start on Saturdays. Saturday morning you had to get all your clothes ironed and ready for church on Sunday. Then Saturday afternoons, all the boys would get haircuts, and when I was old enough, I started my own haircutting business, where I charged fifty cents a haircut. Then on Saturday night, my mother and all the women would come to our house. This included my aunts, cousins, and some women from the neighborhood. We would prepare food for cooking. My mother would create the menu, and everyone else would decide on who was going to prepare what. In the kitchen, someone was always busy cutting the potatoes or seasoning the meat. While we were cooking, we always sang church songs.

At a normal Sunday dinner, we would be feeding twenty to thirty people, so we had to make a lot of food. The women of the house made things like candied yams, collard greens, macaroni and cheese, chicken, chicken and dumplings, okra, gumbo, homemade biscuits, rice and gravy, corn bread, potato salad, sweet potato pies, peach cobbler, coconut cake, chocolate cake, jelly cake, and occasionally red velvet cake. It was always a huge spread, and nothing was ever store-bought. The soul sisters did the food preparation, and we enjoyed fellowshipping while we worked.

I learned the value of work at an early age.

My father was an entrepreneur in the family. He had a business called Jet Enterprise. He would go through the community and offer to help people haul things or move things to the dumpster during the week. On Saturday evenings, the men would wash and clean the truck. Then on Sundays, with the same truck, he would go around the neighborhood and pick up all the kids on Broderick Street to take them to church. Our church was on Fillmore and Ellis in San Francisco, so on Sunday mornings, you dressed up in your Sunday best and rode in the back of my father's hauling truck to church. When our church held their yearly picnic, my father would take the same truck and drive it around the neighborhood to pick up people to take to the picnic.

My father used to say that you've got to be thankful that you are closed in your right mind and that you are still there. This means that you are still capable of thinking in your right mind and you have reasonable health and strength. He used to say that in spite of any illness, handicaps, or disabilities, if you are breathing, then you have reasonable health and strength.

Because of my father's entrepreneurial spirit, I learned that hard work feeds your soul and gives you a healthy spirit. By the time I was eleven, I had started my own little laundry business, which I kept until I was fourteen years old. My grandmother taught me how to iron so clothes didn't have "cat faces," which meant wrinkles. I would go through the neighborhood and collect all the men's work shirts and Sunday shirts. I would hand wash them over a tub, Niagara Starch them, hang them on the line to dry, and then iron them. It was tough work, but I loved it. I would sing straight through my work. I enjoyed it and got money for it. My laundry money helped put food on the table or helped my brothers and sisters with their needs. At age thirteen, I started working because both my parents had it very hard. I started babysitting twelve kids. I would wash clothes, make beds, mop the floor, and cook meals, and I did it all by myself. I always made sure that I had some kind of job.

At age fourteen, I became a candy striper at Mt. Zion Hospital, where I was first introduced to patient care. Then, when I was fifteen, both of my parents had disk problems and were admitted to Kaiser Hospital in Redwood City, where they had back surgery at the same time. That left my older brother and all the kids in the house. At the time, we lived on Bush Street. With my parents not working, we needed money. I saw that there was a convalescent home opening soon. I was only fifteen, but I told the lady that I was seventeen and a half so that I could get the job. I was in high school, so I took the night job. I was assigned to eight patients in the convalescent home. They were ambulatory patients and Alzheimer's was not yet a diagnosis, so we just called the illness a mental disorder. I would feed them snacks and prepare them for bed.

However, before I got the job and when both my parents were already hospitalized, I went to the neighborhood store because there was not much food in the house. My uncles and aunts were on their way to come stay with us, but they had not arrived yet. I went to the corner store to steal a box of grits. I bought some hot dogs, eggs, and bread, but stole the grits. I took that food home and prepared a meal for my brothers and sisters. Later in life, I went back to the store and paid for the food I took. The store owner said he knew that I had stolen the box of grits, but he also knew that I was trying to feed my brothers and sisters, so I hugged and thanked him.

Later, when I was nineteen, I started working as a medical assistant in the OB-GYN department at San Francisco Kaiser Permanente. At that time, there was a family of girls I used to share my clothes with, but I remember this one day, a coworker of mine was in an exam room, putting on makeup. I knew the OB-GYN's Christmas party was a big, important party and that she wanted to look her best and impress everyone. The party was going to be held at the chief's house on Lake Street. I could tell how important the party was to her, and I also knew that I had some nice clothes that would look perfect on her. I knew she didn't have a lot of extra money, but I also understood that as an African American woman, I had to be sensitive and not offend her.

It took me a few days to mention that I had some clothes to share, so she decided to come to my house to see what I had to share. With my mother, we went through all the clothes we had, and she found a purple velvet dress with white lace trim on the long sleeves. She was in heaven when she saw the dress. She took it, along with a red leather trench coat that also looked great on her. By being able to reach out beyond myself and share what I had, I was able to make my coworker happy, and my soul was touched.

My religion is very important to me. It is one thing to be raised with your parents' beliefs, and it's another to finally experience that connection. Although I was baptized as a Baptist around age eight, I didn't have my first real experience of that connection to a higher power until I was about fifteen years old. I attended a weeklong revival at our church. On Friday night there was a special ministry for the youth of the church. The minister talked to us about things that I was dealing with at the time in my life like school, puberty, peer pressure, and learning to stand on your own. He encouraged us to use our parents as role models and reminded us that our body is a temple just as it says in the Bible. Though there were about eighty youth in the audience, it felt like the minister was speaking directly to me. It was such an emotional experience for me that I recognized for the first time in my life that I felt connected spiritually. From that point on, I knew that I wanted to grow stronger in my faith and I wanted to experience this spiritual connection.

I do believe in a higher power, and I have a relationship with a higher power. I had a blood clot in my left calf in 1973 and almost died. I had six more clots after that. Through the power of prayer and faith in my higher power I am still alive. I believe that prayer is a sustainer, and it keeps you going, even when it feels like you just can't go anymore. My higher power is my protector. In my beliefs, if tragedy hits the family, then we simply pray through it. We pray together or individually. We pray at night and give thanks in the morning when we get up. Prayer and faith are strong forces in my life.

I value my husband of almost forty years. He is a great friend and partner. I value my children. I look at them and see them getting older every day. You do your best to lay a solid foundation in faith for your children and pray that they will continue and grow in that faith. My daughter has an eye condition that causes deterioration in her vision. When she was sixteen years old, the doctors told her that she would be blind by the time she was twenty-one. She is now thirty-five, and although her vision is still deteriorating, she can still see. My son, who is thirty-nine, and my daughter have continued to grow spiritually and have a strong faith from both my husband's and my spirituality, and I see them pass that same strength of faith to their family. Both my son and daughter have the faith and spirituality that we hoped to instill in them. We do believe that children rebirth themselves after they leave home, but we were hoping that they would reach beyond themselves and reach out to someone else. They have done so, and I treasure that. I believe that this in itself is success.

The most difficult thing I have had to face was going on a four-day cruise to Mexico with my husband. When we boarded the ship, I told my husband that I was not feeling quite right. I knew that something was wrong, and I thought I was seasick. When we got back to San Francisco, I told my husband to take me to the hospital. I went in to see the doctor and told him that my thigh and my leg were both hurting. The doctor examined me, and a nurse who I thought was a friend said to him, "There's nothing wrong with her." However, the doctor's opinion and the diagnoses differed. He said that I had an ectopic pregnancy. I was taken to the ER. There I saw another doctor, who told me that they had called my family. One of the doctors that I had worked with in the clinic was crying, and she said it was serious. She said the ectopic pregnancy had burst and that I also had a collapsed lung. My husband and my mother arrived, and I was having difficulty breathing. They were crying, and I just started praying.

Shortly after, I started being able to breathe a little bit better. I reminded them of our faith. I knew that my prayers would be answered. In my prayers, I had found peace that only God can provide. He is the sustainer of life and is without judgment. I was very blessed to survive the surgeries and happy to be among the land of the living, to be able to breathe and to smile about it and not let anyone or anything take that away from me. I know what it is like to have a second chance. I know what it is like to look deep in your soul and say, "It is well with my soul." With all the pain, all the drama that life experiences have to offer you, if you are still here, life is good. Life is going through a journey.

I am an active ministry leader at my church. I am connected to my church and to my family through my faith, but that faith also helps me to connect with strangers. When connecting with people I don't know, my faith allows me to be approachable. A lot of times I say to people I pass on the street, "It's going to be okay." Then I wonder why I said that, but that is the spiritual side of being certain. I remember one day, while I was driving my daughter's bag of baby clothes to Goodwill, I saw a mother on the street with a four-year-old and a baby in a stroller. The children weren't wearing hats or snow buntings, and it was very cold. I pulled the car over next to them and said, "Hi. I know you don't know me, but I have these wonderful baby clothes, and I'd like to give them to you." The mother just cried and said, "Thank you." Even though

I didn't know her, it was through my faith that I was able to reach out to her without fear. It is through that same faith that she accepted without question. That is what being a soul sister means to me.

I'm incredibly grateful to God and my parents for all the lessons I learned about opening our home and sharing our lives with others. Their openness and strength has been passed down to my brothers and sisters and me. I'm blessed to have a husband who shares the same welcoming open spirit. We have continued being able to pass on all that we have been given, and have found that we always have more than we need by being open to sharing. My brothers and sister often laugh and joke about how much we've continued in our parents' footsteps and how much joy and happiness living in that faith has brought to us. Without realizing it, we have all continued to pass the same openness and generosity of spirit on to our children. Then I watch as our children share that same love with their children. I see that God is great and that I am truly blessed.

Mary Eliza Mahoney

Mary Eliza Mahoney was born in Boston, Massachusetts, in 1845. Mary expressed an interest in nursing from the time she was a teenager. Because of this interest, she decided to work at the New England Hospital for Women and Children in Roxbury, Massachusetts. She was a cook, janitor, washerwoman, and unofficial nurse's aide for the next fifteen years of her life. In March 1878, at the age of thirty-three, she was admitted to the nursing program at the New England Hospital for Women and Children. Mary Mahoney was one of four, receiving her nursing certification on August 1, 1879, making her the first African- American in history to earn a professional nursing license. Mary Mahoney has received many honors since her death. Mary was inducted into the American Nurses Association's Hall of Fame in 1976. Mary Mahoney will always be remembered and play an important part of history. She is revered in the nursing profession not just for being the first African-American nurse to graduate, but for helping to establish high standards of practice and character for nurses in years to come.

Mahoney, Mary Eliza. Biography. Accessed March 31, 2011.
http://www.asu.edu/nursing/sourses/nur361/leader13/bioigraphy.html

INTRODUCING SOUL SISTER JEAN JONES

INTERESTINGLY ENOUGH, I FIRST MET Jean Jones in the San Francisco OB-GYN department that is now called "Women's Health." This is the same department where Arrenia Corbin and I were medical assistants. Jean was hired as the medical secretary for the department. Since my boss was the chief of the department, we had the opportunity to run into each other a little more than everyone else. She was a strikingly beautiful woman; she had a beautiful figure and always carried herself in a very professional, sophisticated manner. She always remained me of Lena Horne, the singer and actress of the silver screen. She was very quiet and a top-notch secretary. I knew that to be true because my boss would have never hired anyone who was not the best in their field. When I left San Francisco, Jean also attended my farewell party, and I felt it was swell of her to care about seeing me off. Although Jean and I were not as close as Arrenia and I, I still liked her all the same because to me she symbolized the utmost in professionalism. I did not know for years to come that our paths would cross again.

I was living with my husband in the Sierra Nevada foothills. I had just been promoted to my second managerial position. I had left the Sonoma County area and transferred to the beautiful little town of Cool, California. My husband had built a home there for a place to retire in the future. Since I was transferred, we could live there, and I could commute to South Sacramento. We had separated two years prior and wanted to give our marriage another try, so we relocated to this area. It proved to be a good decision.

It was in 1993 that I happened to see Jean walking across the staff parking lot at South Sacramento Medical Center. From my car window, I noticed her and got all excited that I had finally seen a familiar face. I tried to find her but could not locate her or the department she worked in. Our relationship took another spin when I was promoted once again and expanded my management and administrative assignments. Without my knowledge, I was the replacement manager for Jean's department in medical secretaries. I was pleased about the additional assignments but kind of worried about how my new appointment would affect my relationship with Jean.

After I completed my master's program in health services administration, my boss felt I was ready to expand my job duties and responsibilities. I now had two offices within our health care facility, and when I moved into my new office in the medical secretary department, Jean seemed a little more quiet than usual; I wanted to change that around. I wanted her to feel comfortable with me and to strike our friendship up again. It took some time to achieve this feat, but before long, Jean and I had returned to a warm and friendly relationship. She began to share with me that she was interested in being promoted to a senior medical secretary within the department and that she had been going to college to get her degree to provide her more opportunity to be ready for promotions.

I felt that there was a need for a senior medical secretary because my assignments and the departments I was managing were increasing. I needed someone to oversee the department when I was absent going to other meetings and visiting the other department, which was a 24-7 responsibility. I received approval for additional funding to have a senior medical secretary job in the department. There was another person in the department who was also interested in the position, but her interactions with the other personnel were at times problematic and I knew there would be more areas of concern if she was hired since we were in a union environment and the union rule was that the one with the most seniority should be the next to be promoted. Jean was the most senior in the department and, in my opinion, the best person in merit and ability to handle complex situations with the membership and customer service issues. It pleased me very much when Jean was awarded the position of senior medical secretary. It was at this time that our relationship and friendship really started to flourish. Finally, I had someone I could depend on to be responsible and professional to handle all situations in the department and to make good judgment calls when I was not there.

As we got to know more about each other during this time, I discovered Jean had raised her sister's baby after her sister's sudden death. I thought to myself what a special lady she must be to have her own struggles in life but to have enough kindness and love in her heart to raise her sister's child. This only added to the high regard I already had for Jean. I do not think she ever realized how much I looked up to her in the years that passed; I truly respected her ability to be at the top of her field as a legal medical secretary. She added greatly to my work career, and I'm so happy our relationship and friendship have stood the test of time.

I was invited to Jean's house the day she and Ron were married. I felt so good about attending and seeing the wonderful smile on Jean's face, full of happiness for her love of Ron. To me they were the perfect couple, so full of happiness. Their light blue and gold trim African American wedding outfits were quite beautiful.

In 2000, I left employment in the Sacramento area and was recruited to the Diablo service area. Jean and I continued to stay in touch with each other.

Through the years, I provided assistance to Jean in her career endeavors. I always thought God had a special plan for us to share. It was not until I thought about writing *Soul Sisters, Come on to My House* that I would know just what the plan was.

Many years later, in January 2009, I had a severe head-on car accident. My husband and I spent much time that year in three different health facilities where Jean's human kindness reached out to me. I had been retired for three years when one winter, very foggy day, my husband and I were in a horrific head-on car crash. I came very close to losing my husband and my left arm.

I remember it was when I was admitted into a rehab center that Jean called me and said she would like to come and visit with me. She asked, "What would you like to eat?" We were going to have lunch together, and she was willing to pick me up whatever I wanted. To someone who is in a rehab nursing home, nothing sounds better than a hamburger, fries, and a strawberry shake. It was twelve o'clock, just lunchtime, when Jean met me in the lobby of the rehab center with her fast-food lunch of sheer deliciousness.

She also brought me some gifts. One was a pink, stuffed rabbit holding an orange carrot. To my surprise, I had been missing my little blue stuffed rabbit at home on my bed. I wanted to hug it when I needed to comfort myself, and I was thinking about it now that I was in severe pain and hurting. Well, lo and behold, Jean came through with this little pink rabbit to help keep me company. She never knew how much it meant to me. The pink rabbit comforted me in my loneliness at the rehab center.

After a few weeks, I went to stay with my son in his house in Sacramento recovering until my husband was out of the rehab center. My son had given me a ride to the rehab center to visit with my husband and Jean offered to drive me home one night after I visited him. It was a Friday about eight o'clock, and I was beginning to worry about her because the weather was stormy. Just after eight, Jean came in looking all tired and hurried. Apparently this was one of the Fridays she chose to work, and she had been fighting traffic all this time to reach me. She had gone without dinner, and her only concern was to help me out by giving me a ride home. To me, it was the true sign of a friend and soul sister.

These are the many reasons I selected Jean as my soul sister, and it was not until after she shared her life story that I realized something else after all these years of knowing her. I realized that she is a deep thinker, who has the capacity to think beyond herself and understand life's struggles with compassion and understanding. Her story is one that is genuine and goes to the deepest depths of the soul.

"I HAD TO DO IT ON MY OWN"
by Jean Jones

MY NAME IS JEAN JONES. I was born December 15, 1952, in San Francisco, California. I lived all my life in San Francisco except the last nineteen years in Sacramento, California. I have a bachelor of science degree in business from California State University of Sacramento. I'm age fifty-seven now and moved from San Francisco in my early forties. As an infant, I lived in Navy Row for a couple of years. Then my mom moved to the Western Additions, which is over by Eddy Street and the Divisadero; we lived there for a couple of years. It seems like for the first nine years of my life, we moved around a lot—from Hunters Point, to the Bayview, to the Fillmore area—until I was nine years old, and then we moved to the Lakeview area in San Francisco.

I remember starting elementary school there maybe two years before I went to middle school. All this was occurring around the mid-1960s. There was a lot going on during that period. I had my first boyfriend in middle school. I think I was about thirteen years old when I started middle school. That was just a few years before a lot of blacks started to come to my school. I went to school there before integration started. At one point, the middle school was totally Caucasian. I remember having a hard time with some of the instructors there. I was kind of flippant; if you said something out of place to me, I would tell you how I felt. I remember telling one white teacher something really nasty. I kind of felt bad about it later, but she made me really mad. At that time blacks were kind of getting acclimated. I was getting too acclimated to middle school and the freedom to wear what you wanted. Before that, the dress in elementary school was very traditional. You could not wear pants at either school, elementary or middle school. But I remember I could now wear short dresses, and I remember hemming all my dresses so I thought I was a real big girl when I started middle school. I guess I was starting to feel my oats a little bit.

I remember meeting my first boyfriend, named Ray. He had eight brothers and one sister, and we were pretty close. We used to love listening to music. It was during the time when James Brown was really popular, and we used to say, "Say it loud. I'm black, and I'm proud," because it was that whole 1960s thing going on. The music with James Brown was more popular to me than any other. Before him it was the Temptations and the Supremes, but he was kind of out of the mold. He was more race-conscious, and we used to listen to a lot of his music. Although my boyfriend and I were good friends, we were still pretty innocent. We were just having a relationship, and I was only thirteen or fourteen years old when we went together.

When I graduated from middle school, I went to Abraham Lincoln High School and got pregnant. Before I got pregnant, there was something going on in my family. My family had a lot of disconnects. My mom and dad were having their own issues because my stepfather was very controlling and not connected to the family at all. His only interest was to look good and things had to look good too. The house had to look good and my stepfather was very materialistic, but as far as family, there was a disconnect. I guess he worked the 3:00 p.m. to 11:00 p.m. shift, so he was not home most of the time. My mom did not work for years, but when they bought a home together, she had to go to work and help pay for the cost of raising a family. She'd had three children of her own before they got together. Before they even married, they had all their children together, which consisted of eight children.

The dynamics between my mother and stepfather were just crazy. He was a womanizer; and looking back on those years later, I realized because of the things he would do to me that he was a pedophile. I thought I was getting attention from him, and what he was actually doing was sexually molesting me, especially touching me in inappropriate places. He would tickle me, and we would all be in bed together—my mom, me, and him. He would be tickling me, but he was touching my breasts at the same time. I remember once he grabbed a pillow like he was going to suffocate me. It was years later that I realized what had happened and how panicky that made me. Some experiences in my adulthood brought back those memories. For example, I would go under the water when I was swimming, and I could not stay under there for very long because I could not catch my breath. I could not get enough air because I was panicking. That is something I still struggle with today.

The dynamics of my life at home were really, really bad. I had three brothers at home. I had three younger sisters, and I was the oldest and many times was left at home to care for my brothers and sisters. My parents would go out and go grocery shopping and not take all the children with them. Even my mother, before she got together with him, she had at least five children she was raising on her own pretty much. I was the caregiver for them. She was a young woman, and she still wanted to go out. Ever since I was five or six years old, I was often left behind to take care of my brothers and sisters. I remember being very young taking clothes to get wash and taking care of the house. I was always kind of a "little mother," and that role has always kind of stuck with me throughout my life.

I have been really trying to step out of that character, but this role has been a real challenge for me because I tend to still mother my brothers, sisters, and their children today. I have had to step back and question whether this is something I really want to continue. They've made their own lives and they have to deal with the consequences of this; I have tried to allow them to do this regardless of how it makes me feel.

So the challenges and dynamics of growing up in my family really caused me to suppress a lot of my own feelings. There was a time in my family when I was very mouthy. I would say what I thought and what I saw. I always thought I was very insightful because I could see things that I would say to my mom, especially about my stepfather. She would always talk to him about what I saw. I even talked to her about how he was behaving toward me because it was not just me but my younger sister as well. My mom did not do anything. I used to think that maybe all families are like this and maybe this is something all families go through. I just learned how to take care of myself. All I could do was to take care of myself in this situation because I really did not have my mother there for me.

What I realized later on in my life was that I was really a neglected little girl. The only time that I was cared for was when I spent time with my grandparents. My real father was angry at my mother. When she was pregnant with me, he contracted a disease, and he thought I was not his child. So I had to live with that in my family, especially on my dad's side. After I was born, he joined the army for two terms. He was probably there for about six years, and I would see him now and again when I was at my grandmother's, his mother's. She kind of stepped in and took care of me with her husband, my grandfather. My grandfather was the most positive role model in my family; although he was an alcoholic, at least he showed some concern for me. He cared about me.

I had so much of men trying to come on to me in my life; a lot of men would say I was very attractive. I felt ugly, and I did not have any self-esteem. It got progressively worse as I got older. I would just walk down the street, and men would make catcalls at me; it was so humiliating, I would just want to hide in a closet. I did not have a very good self-image. Now that I'm older, I wish I had all that attention, but at that time it did not feel good. I used to think, *Oh, I will be so glad when I get older. I will not have to deal with this.* I thought I could get past all this and not have to deal with the craziness.

In my home, my three younger brothers had their bedrooms downstairs. But it was a bar most times on the weekends because they would have their friends over there. These guys would get drunk. Then they would make passes at me and say stupid stuff to me. Everywhere I went, there was something to deal with.

I think when you are growing up it feels like you kind of live in a closed neighborhood. You do not have a television or the media like today, but you really do not know what is going on outside of your neighborhood. So you are just kind of living within your community, and if you have all these dynamics going on—this kind of dysfunction going on, you are pretty much consumed with all of that. I think there were many other families consumed with that as well, with issues of economics, issues of racism, and issues dealing with your own civil rights. I think many black people did have these concerns, but it is only my own perspective because I was very young. I would think about all of that. You would kind of stay within your own community, and you kind of stayed within that close-knit group. It is kind of like everybody had their own issues. They would party and have a good time so they did not have to think about the dynamics of what was going on. They all went to their jobs, and when they came home, they had to make sure they had a roof over their heads, clothing for themselves and their children, and enough money to pay for the utilities. They concentrated more about the things they were more familiar with.

In my family, they would tell you about education, but when I see my parents today, I realize how inept they were then in parenting skills. They came through something themselves; they did not have their parents there for them. They were abandoned children, and so they were just in a survival mode. They were just trying to survive, and so there was no psychological connecting when they told you to get an education; they were not "walking the walk and talking the talk." They were trying to get some ground themselves, and they were trying to get some stability themselves. They kept having all these children, and they did not know how to meet all the needs of their children.

The valuable thing I got from my family was learning to take care of myself financially. I had to look after myself. I learned how to manage my money and how to manage my household because I saw my grandmother doing that. I saw my dad's mother as a very strong woman with her money. She always helped her children. She was from Homer, Louisiana. She was actually from a different place in Louisiana, but she settled in Homer with her husband. Her husband's family was well off; they had their own plantation and land. They had doctors and lawyers in their family, but the husband she married became abusive and mentally ill. Therefore, she left him and went to California. This was during a time when there was a war, and lots of folks were moving to California because there were jobs available. When she left her children behind, she had three sons and three daughters. One daughter and son were twins.

When she went to California, she took on the responsibility of getting her home and house together. She lived in Hunters Point in San Francisco, and slowly she got her children to move out here too. She saved her money and bought a nice, big home. We always saw my grandmother as wealthy because she had her own nice, big home and was well taken care of. I would go and spend summers with her. She would buy me anything I wanted, and it would just be that she would nurture me. My father's mother was very fair; she had long gray hair, and she would go to the beautician and get it dyed purple. She was a very sophisticated lady. She told me that her father was Irish and her mother was from Africa, probably mixed with Indian. My dad was very fair because his father was very fair, and he had Spanish in him so my dad looked Spanish. Jones is my maiden name, and it kind of sounds Spanish. I have read history books, and I know the Spanish had slaves in the South. I'm sure they had a slave that was Spanish on my dad's side. On my mother's side, they were a darker race. She has my complexion. My grandfather had American Indian in him, and he was really tall, dark, and thin. My grandmother probably had more African in her, so you know it is really a hodgepodge going through my veins.

Getting back to finances, I have remained truthful to my beliefs. I have always been financially responsible. It was the role I had to play in my family, but it also was the role I played to take care of my children. I have done that on an economic level, but I have missed the mark in raising my children because I was psychologically unable. I had my own mental illness. I was kind of numb and unavailable emotionally, but I went through the motions of what I had to do as a parent. The disconnect I got from my parents went over into my role as a parent. My daughter has always been the type of person who has kept me thinking because she would always tell me what she thought. I had the courage to stop and think about what she said to me. I think it was her ability and my love for her that really helped me to be a good parent. I wanted to be a good parent. I wanted to be a better parent than my own parents were to me. We always say this, but I started to look like my own parents and my own stepfather before I got help. I thought I was doing a better job emotionally, but I was not connected. In many ways, I abandoned my daughter emotionally, because I was just out there in the world trying to fix myself with my relationships with men. I have never had a stable relationship with men or any of my dads. Although I had a grandfather, he was an alcoholic, so how much could he really give me? My mother gave me what she could, but she had all these kids, and she also had a husband who was unplugged in that relationship that was always causing havoc. He was financially stable and a good provider; he bought her material things. So what she had in her, she gave to this man and neglected her children. Unfortunately this still goes on today.

I would like to share with you what I think about my people and their culture. They are real characters, and they are so diverse and so different. I think it is really just like all of us. But if I think about my culture, I think about colors of oranges, yellows, greens—very bright colors. I think about art, that deep expression of art flourishing so vibrantly. I think about love because they are earthy people. When you think about the earth, they are so grounded and connected to the land. I think about their suffering. I think about the pathology of their suffering but their endurance. I think about their ability to overcome and their strength. They are spiritual. Then there are those you know who become lost, get angry, and become perpetrators. So there are some who get lost, some will make it, and some will not.

In regard to my immediate family, we used to have picnics. The family would gather with others and have barbeques; we would go to the water and swim. Friends would get together, and we would have big fish fries. They would go out on boats and bring home the fish and fry it up. So the kids would all be together, and they would play together. The parents would be all together, and they would party together. Family was special. My mom on all the holidays would get together with others and cook all this food. She is a great cook and she still does this, but unfortunately that thing with alcohol is present. Alcohol does not do anything but make things worse, but there was always a sense of family and a sense of gathering. There was always a sense of gathering together with friends and family, and there was always lots of food. We would have gumbo and fried shrimp and fish, especially snapper. Sometimes we would have chitterlings, greens, corn bread, lots of sweet potato pie, and lots of cakes, such as Seven-Up cakes.

My great-grandmother was a great cook, and she would make pound cake that would just melt in your mouth. She was my mother's mother, and I lived with her for a while too, right after my daughter was born. She helped me a lot with my daughter. She too was an alcoholic and turned out not to be very religious. She used to go to church all the time, and she used to take me to church when I was a little girl. However, I think her alcoholism got the best of her so she stopped going to church. During the week she would drink, and so when it was time to go to church, she could no longer hide the alcohol on her breath. She didn't want to be in the presence of churchgoers in that way, so slowly she left the ministry. Maybe there were other things going on at that time; but I just know she stopped going to church.

After that she got more into alcohol, and then she had a husband. He would live with her, and then he would leave, and then he would live with her again. He would have a girlfriend on the side, with whom I used to live at one time. I really think about the dynamics of the relationships of these men and women, and I think maybe it could go back to Africa. Because in Africa they did have many wives, and the women pretty much took care of the household together with other women. I think some of it came from slavery. I think about how the families were broken off and sold from one another, and so it is a history of abandonment. I think some of this is a residual from all of that. As a result of slavery, some families were so splintered, so out of kilter, that they were just not able to have a family life. They tried and they tried hard, but there was so much psychological pain and emotional hurt going on then. It is only now when there is help out there that we can make those changes. The impact of it was so severe and so damaging, it just permeated historically throughout the family.

Thinking of Jean's point of view, I mentioned, "I think you raise a very insightful perspective about this: because there was so much pain and hurt because of the separation of families, it almost did not pay to get attached on a deep level. With the total uncertainty, it almost didn't pay to have a strong relationship with someone because you did not know from one moment to the next when all that was going to be taken away from you. This makes sense to me because now, almost two hundred years later when there is no fear of slavery, we are back to families again and gatherings and having this unity again, so something had to come in the way to change all that. Unfortunately, your parents were an outcome of all of that, and somehow they lost their way. Your generation has a tendency to bring it back together again. That is a very interesting statement to describe this way of life."

I do not drink much because I saw too much. My stepfather would serve teenagers drinks; he had no boundaries. Many of my brothers and sisters are alcoholics today because of it. I know I just could not handle it because I have other things I had to do besides drugs and alcohol. I didn't think I could do all that and get up the next day and go to work too. My mother would have blackouts every once in a while. I would say something to her the next day about something she did, and she did not recall it. I did not understand the term "blackouts" then, and I could not understand why she could not remember what she did the night before. Sometimes she would go to bed and then get up and go to the kitchen to warm something up. A couple of times, the kitchen caught on fire.

Most of my life, I was looking for love, but what I really needed to do was learn how to love myself. I kept hitting the same roadblocks in relationships. I always ended up hurt and in pain. I was not getting my needs met but always trying to meet the needs of someone else. I had to learn to ask for what I wanted and make sure my needs were met. It's not just sexual, but in so many other ways. I mention sexual being a person who has been raped and having to deal with a lot of sexual abuse from men verbally and physically in my home and on the job in a lot of different places. I did not know how to get my own sexual needs met; I thought my body was there for them. I did not have a very good body image, and I was not connected to my body. I was not in touch with my body, and it was not until I got to the place where I was in too much pain, I was suffering, and my sister died—it was like that was it. I needed to look at what was going on because I could no longer become this victim or play a victim role, always putting myself in a way that I was the victim. When you are always setting yourself up to be the victim, you have an inkling that something is not right but you go into it anyway and everything about you is a victim.

When my sister died, I was in great pain. I went into therapy and the twelve-step program. Looking at all that stuff and reading self-help books like *Women Who Love Too Much*, I finally learned that I was responsible for me. I wanted to stop looking for someone else through men. I was looking for a mother, and I was looking for a father. I started to look to myself for parenting myself. Once I started to look at it from that point, it took lots and lots of years for me to change my thoughts. It did not happen overnight or in one year or two years; it was a slow, progressive process for me because there were so many things rooted in my behavior. I was so rooted in being the victim. I was so rooted in thinking that someone needed to be responsible for me because there were people in my family saying, "You need to get married; you need to get a man." So I was out there looking for a man to take care of me, and then there was this physical abuse and I needed to do something or I was going to die. I did not want to die; I had children.

My sister was a year younger than I. We had a very tumultuous relationship growing up. In some ways, we were close; and in other ways, we were not, due to jealousy. When I think back, I remember I had a grandmother who was there for me, and she did not have that. Because we had different fathers, we did not have the same grandmother to step in and nurture her, and there was some animosity there. I was the caregiver, being the oldest child and giving all the orders all the time. She did not want me to be telling her what to do all the time. I think there was some bitterness from her to me, but I always tried to be there for her. My sister was very young when she ran away from home. She was probably about fourteen or fifteen, and my parents did not go out looking for her; they just let her go and stay out in the street. She connected with some guy and then went on heroin and got pregnant by some guy. Her first child was addicted to heroin, and that was a tragedy. Even today, that son has such a hard time. Then she got involved with another guy, and she got pregnant by him. I think she stopped using heroin, but it had an effect on the child. Three weeks after he was born, she died. We knew she was a heroin addict, and we thought maybe that had something to do with it. When finally the autopsy report came in, it said she died of asthma and bronchitis.

I never knew she had asthma and bronchitis, but that is what is on her death certificate; it was not an overdose. She was living with an older man, who was not the father of the child. Her first son was probably seven years old when she died. His grandfather took him and raised him for a time. However, he came to live with me for a year when he was five years old.

He was my sister's son, and I bonded with him right away; it was a baby that needed to be cared for, and it was always my mode to be a caretaker. My mother did not want to take care of him, and his other grandmother did not want to take care of him. His father was a merchant seaman and did not want to take care of him. He even said he was not his son. I remember my stepfather saying, "If you take on this responsibility, do not expect any help from anyone." I was twenty-nine at the time this happened. I eventually received a guardianship for him. His father died a few years later, so we eventually received Social Security for him for a long time, until he was eighteen. Once I got guardianship, he was on my health plan. I did not know if I was doing the right thing for myself, for him, and even for my daughter. My daughter eventually said to me, "Why are you taking on all these kids?" She said this when his brother came to live with us and I was beginning to neglect her. I was asking her to help me because I was taking classes and she needed to take care of Mark. She was twelve years old, and I was putting a heavy burden on her. Life started to repeat itself. I think at the time, there was some resentment. I took him to the doctor, and he was diagnosed with ADHA. He was kind of out of control at school. He got progressively worse.

When we moved to Sacramento, I was on my own with him, and things got worse. I was at my wits' end with him. It was hard and tough. I began to say, "I cannot do this anymore, Mark, because you are driving me crazy." So he was starting to feel like he was not wanted because no one else was there for him but me. It was so out of control that I could not do it anymore. You love someone, but you know there is some resentment there. My sister was gone, and she left this child with problems.

This is where I believe the most important thing about life is that you can get through it in spite of anything. You can really do it regardless of your highs and your lows. Regardless of whatever you are going through in life, you can get through it. If you connect with the spiritual part of you with meditation and prayer, if you connect with something outside of yourself and really trust that the power greater than you is going to help you get through it, then you can make it. You can really make it. You may go through some lows, but you can later say, "I wanted to die, but I kept going." What kept me going is I did not want to leave my children; there was something to live for. I did not have a right to be that selfish. It's like today you might feel so stressed, you go to sleep or take a nap, and you wake up and get a whole different perspective on things—you can get your energy back.

I do not care how painful or how down you may feel, you can get through it one day at a time. Sometimes all you can take is "one moment at a time." Sometimes that is all you can do, but just take that moment at a time. Just take that moment, and then just take another moment.

I was asked by Susan Korn, a woman I've known over the years beginning around 1980, to participate with her and other diverse women to write our stories, including our work history. It's been over a year since I've been toying with this whole idea. I started writing of the experiences I've had in my family and the effects they've had on my behavior. Of course, when some of us talk about our families and there has been some abuse, we always start with the unfortunate events that I have come to know have significantly impacted my behavior in all aspects of my decisions and subsequent experiences. Yet because of a more recent experience and because this book is about diversity on the job and how change needs to happen, I have been motivated to intertwine life experience and job experience and show how they intertwine.

As soon as I mentioned change, a green light flashed under the word *change* in the preceding sentence, so it's time, whether others want to accept it or not, change is needed. Those who want things to be the same will be left behind, and it certainly will divide the country. A narrow view of the country or continuing the status quo will cause a tremendous rift in this country, and it may turn out to be very ugly. We cannot grow and continue to do the same thing; I don't think it fits into any positive model. I don't recall during the depression that there was a civil war, but the people came through, probably for the better. Well, as we come through our economic crisis, change will need to happen; otherwise, we may not be able to come through another economic crisis without tremendous impact.

This is where I come in with my insight why change needs to happen in the workforce. I have worked in California and specifically in San Francisco and Sacramento for at least forty years, and in one organization for over thirty years. With that amount of time under my feet, my insight carries a lot of weight and validity. When I initially started out working at a well-known HMO, I had no intentions of working there this long; it has now been over thirty years. My intentions were to work during the summer and then start classes in the fall, but being a single parent, I had responsibilities and what started out as a summer job eventually became a permanent one. I wanted to go back to school and change my career, but I ended up working full-time and attended evening classes. I'm always seeking a better way to make a living, with my motive being to do something that would be valuable to others and me; however, when City College of San Francisco closed down for the summer of 1978, probably for monetary reasons, I decided to get a job. With my mother's encouragement, I applied at a well-known HMO. I was hired immediately and started working as a temporary employee whose job would be up by the end of the summer. I enjoyed working in the administration department as a typist during that summer. I worked with two people that were a joy to work with. Both of those people are now deceased, but we had a good time working together and we laughed. There was laughter on the job, something I think is essential on the job—otherwise the business won't survive. I think another important ingredient you need is to be open to others' ideas and what others have to offer, even though it looks so different from what is familiar.

My first job started in late 1970 or early 1971. I was seventeen years old and was the mother of a young child. There were so many things going on during this time in my personal life and in the nation. I got my first job at a well-known bank. It was during a time when the Civil Rights Movement had opened the door to working downtown in an office building, instead of cleaning the floors, and I worked as a secretary. During this time, I had so much going on and, looking back, I see it was grace that brought me through. Months before, my stepfather had told me to leave within a week, and my mother stood by and let it happen. What precipitated this action was my refusal to give into his demands. Although I lived in his household, I never had a key to the front door and whenever they weren't home to let me in, I had to wait outside until they returned. I lived in an environment where my care and nurturing were sacrificed for the sake of others. I became the adult very early in life, and when I was no use to either of my parents, I was told to leave. My stepfather tried to date me; my mother, despite what I was telling her very early in my youth, didn't know how to protect me. When my mother was in her early twenties, she was on welfare and the single parent of six children—three by my stepfather, who was married and at that time had six other children by at least three other women.

I was kicked out, but fortunately I found out about a program opening up to help blacks get jobs. I interviewed for the program. Initially I wasn't chosen; however, someone backed out, leaving an opening for me. The training course and tests were for at least two to three months, and then we were placed in a department.

I did well in the program, and eventually I was placed in the steno pool and subsequently as a secretary in the trust department. I had learned secretarial skills while in high school and was a good typist, and those skills were helpful but I needed to improve. I hadn't graduated from high school and needed to continue to grow, so I took the GED tests and passed the first time, with high scores in comprehension. I eventually took night classes at City College, and in the meantime, I was living with my great-grandmother, who was taking care of my daughter. While working at the bank, my skills were average but improving. While there, I knew I was being monitored, but I was naïve and ignorant about civil rights, racism, and the ways of the world, and I kept my feelings to myself. I needed a job, and I didn't have time to think much about those things. There were times when those in authority would act hatefully, but I just went about doing my job as best I could—plus I didn't have anyone to turn to so, like my family, I held it in and pushed forward. The bank on the whole was decent, and I worked there for approximately two years until I married and quit. During my time with the bank, the building didn't get blown up, the company didn't go bankrupt, and I wasn't creating havoc or taking revenge for the deeds of those who feared me. I worked, I paid my bills, I went to school, and I did my best to raise my daughter.

I married a man whom I had known for many years, but only as a family/friendship relationship. The marriage didn't last any longer than this sentence. I quit my good bank job, moved out of my apartment in a good neighborhood, and moved to Germany with him. A month later, he got psychologically sick. While in Germany, I lived with a German family, but I could not speak their language. My daughter was about three years old, and they had a couple of young children. They would all play together. I was there for about a month before I came back to California. My husband had gotten very ill and was in the hospital, so we had to come back to California sooner than we had anticipated; we had planned to be there for at least a year. When he became ill, armed forces sent him back to the States, and I followed later.

The German family I lived with was nice and treated my daughter well. I'd go and sit with them at times, and I would try to communicate the best we could. Their little girls would come up and ask me to fix them some scrambled eggs; they always liked their scrambled eggs with catsup. It was a different and very good experience for me. When my husband was ill and I had no one to take me to the hospital, I had to hitchhike and take trains that were miles away. The trains were so slow and it was such a faraway place and I had to do it on my own. It would take me an hour or two to get where I was going, and sometimes it took me even longer to get back. I thought later, *How did I have the courage to do that then?* But back then, I had more courage than I have today. When I think back, I just had to do what I had to do. I did it, and I put fear aside. We came back to the States and after spending several months in a psych ward, he was released to resume his duties in the armed forces. He was stationed in Tacoma, Washington, where my daughter and I moved to be with him. It was several months later that I left him, fleeing for my life because of physical abuse.

I moved in with my maternal great-grandmother after returning from Tacoma, Washington. My daughter and I lived with my great-grandmother for about eight months and I then moved out into my own apartment. I had more baggage, but I had to keep moving on. I got another job, set up housekeeping, and went back to school. By this time I was working for an investment company where some nasty and embarrassing questions were being asked such as "What's it like living in the ghetto?" On another occasion during a Christmas party another broker asked me if I would go to bed with him and he would pay me. I had very limited interaction with these men and to come out of nowhere with this stuff only cause me to withdraw and feel alone. These remarks were humiliating and I actually wanted to quit but I had responsibilities. I didn't file complaints because I felt it would not have mattered. I was the only black person and I felt very alienated. Of course, they knew I came from the ghetto because I was black and a single parent. Yes, I didn't have money, but whatever my parents were lacking in parenting, they had done one thing, and that was to provide financially for their family. I had lived in a home that my parents bought when I was eleven years old, and I had gone to good schools. I remember being a bright student, loving spelling and math. My paternal grandmother, with whom I spent a great deal of time growing up, owned her own home and helped her children buy their homes. My biological father was a real estate broker who was working to make a million dollars. He bought property, as did his brothers, and so our family was doing well. To assume I was just some black girl from the backwoods was an assumption that is so often made by whites. I was humiliated and confounded by the remarks, and I recall just leaving the office feeling hurt and bewildered.

I lived with my alcoholic grandmother until I got my own place, but my daughter continued to be under her care while I worked. If it wasn't for my great-grandmother, I just don't know how my life would have turned out at this point. In fact, I had two grandmothers: my biological dad's mother and my great-grandmother, who raised my mother, both loved me when I needed it. I wasn't getting love at home; there was too much abuse. My mother was being abused, my brothers were being abused, and I was being sexually assaulted. I never had sex with him, but there was inappropriate touching, and if I had agreed to go to bed with him, he would have had no remorse. When I got out of that house, I had nightmares for years, and when I woke from those nightmares, I was so relieved I was in my own place. It was an emotional nightmare living with my parents. We had pretty things and a pretty home, but where was the love? Many of my siblings are still suffering, covering it up with drugs, hate, loneliness, anger, and so many other useless habits, but I'm striving.

In regard to schooling, when I took the GED, it was my high scores in comprehension that helped me. My math was lacking at that point. It had been a few years since I was in school, but I passed and that was all that mattered. I eventually started taking classes at City College of San Francisco. My great-grandmother took on the mothering of my daughter while I worked and took classes in the evening. I have always strived to be more and have more, but more than that, working and going to school kept me sane. It kept me from being idle and getting into mischievous behavior. There were men in my life, but I always seemed to gravitate toward men who resembled my parents so they weren't lasting relationships because they became abusive. I was looking for love, but I ended up with something other than that; because I didn't love myself, I didn't know what real love looked like. I know now that I needed to have been learning how to love myself.

Working and taking classes didn't give me much time to be with my daughter, and it was my great-grandmother that provided that help, for which I will always be grateful. Although she was an alcoholic, she loved my daughter and took care of her, and my daughter has fond memories of her great-great-grandmother, Agnes.

I left the job before my present employer because I was in an accident, and the opportunity to go out on disability was prompted by the man who was my boss and a stockbroker running his own department. This is the same man who sexually harassed me after a Christmas party, trying to buy sex. I was again humiliated, had nowhere to turn, and went back to work after the ordeal. I couldn't see that I had any rights, and I was young. There was no one around on the job that I could tell who I felt would be the least bit interested. In fact, after he made these remarks, it was a few months later I started working for him. I was hired to work with the house attorney, but I didn't meet his standards and so I was pushed off into the department where investments were made in new offerings. I was reading to get my broker's license, but that was cut short by some higher-up, and so I moved into the bond department. I don't recall what got me there, but this is the bond broker who tried to buy sex from me earlier at the Christmas party. I was the only woman in the department and the only black person in the entire firm. I needed a job—what else was I going to do? I worked there until I couldn't go any further, and when the opportunity to go to school and be home with my daughter came up, I grabbed it.

Unfortunately school was out that summer at City College of San Francisco, so I started working at my present employer with the intention of only being there the summer and then going to school to learn another trade. I had been a secretary since I was seventeen years old and I wanted something more, but the money I was making was helping me make a living and so I started working full-time with benefits, especially medical care—another savior along the way. Again I worked and took night classes; my daughter was older and was able to look after herself and had her father's grandparents helping me at this time. I didn't mention her father because he died when she was six months old; I'm not sure if he would have made that much difference if he had lived because he didn't claim her. I don't know if he believed me at the time of his death from an automobile accident, but I know she was his. Although my first sexual encounter was when I was raped, my second sexual encounter was with him after he had given me a drug, manipulated me into his house, and took advantage. I got pregnant that night in a daze. I hadn't taken any drugs before, so I didn't know how to handle myself. It wasn't until I went into counseling that I realized I had been date raped and I was traumatically stressed out. However, before all that, I went on with life. Looking back, I was living with an abusive stepfather and a mother who was a child herself, and raising a daughter, and being taken advantage of, but I didn't know anything about date rape and so I went on with life. I had to move on because I had a responsibility with a child and I knew I couldn't depend on others. Eventually I got a full-time job, and now thirty years later, I am still here with Kaiser Permanente.

Early in my life I had got it that despite how much I wanted to be cared for, I had to learn how to do it for myself; after all, I had been mothering so early in my youth, I had learned I was responsible. The change that has taken place in me since my childhood is my ability to forgive my parents. I think the most important thing to me over the years is being able to see them as just human beings and to see my own imperfections. That forgiveness has freed me up a lot because I can love them in spite of their behavior. I now have control of how much I want to put into that relationship as far as how much time I want to spend with them. If I'm not feeling comfortable in that environment, I know how to take myself out of that environment. The thing I know now is to have more respect for my feelings and take better care of myself. I realize I'm not a child anymore and that I'm a woman. I do not have to be there anymore at my mother and stepfather's house and feel I need to be nurtured or cared for anymore. I accept them the way they are. I have learned how important it is to take care of myself. When it comes to my children, I am there for them and I support them, but they have to be there for themselves. They have to be the best parent for themselves. I'm there for them, but I cannot do it for them. I have to "parent" myself.

I accept the fact that I have my weaknesses, but I have to continue to look at my strengths. I lived with a family that always made me feel like I was not good enough and that I could not do anything right, that I was weak but I was sensitive. I had no one to really go to with all these feelings, and now that I know how to take care of myself when I'm feeling overwhelmed, I go to a place where I can get what I need. It may mean going to my prayer closet and praying or reading the word, talking to God, or going into therapy. I grab onto everything I need to keep myself in the best state of mind I can, no matter what it takes. Because I grew up in a family that told me, "You do not tell anyone what goes on in your household," I ended up with all these things going on in my head and I got all this pain and suffering; it is like I was about to explode. When I went into therapy, I was about to explode, and going into therapy was the best thing I could do for myself.

My family is important because when it all comes down to it, all we have is family. We need each other during hard times and good times. We need each other for love, comfort, and support. Family does not always have to be your biological family, but it is people that you have that real close relationship with and have an intimate relationship with. To me, one of the most important things is to love each other. We need to learn how to love, and learning how to accept love is what's very important.

As for now, I enjoy working out and exercising. I love dancing, and I love singing. I love to go outdoors on adventures. I am an outdoors person. I love reading, I love learning new things, and I enjoy spending time with friends. I enjoy good food. I enjoy traveling. I wish I had more time and money to travel because I love to see new places and experience different places and people. I'm not much for going to the tourist places because I love being with the natives and locals. I love to talk to the people. So I love traveling, I like to take walks, and I love to walk by the water.

When I think of the word "soul," I think of Aretha Franklin when she is singing her songs. She sings about respecting yourself, about sensitivity, honesty, heart, and soul. It is like that part of you that is so hard to explain that all you can do is express it in some way. You can express it through love, you can express it through music, you can express it through art, and you can express it through relationships. It is a very intimate part of you that is very sensitive, honest, and pure, with lots of emotions too.

A soul sister is someone that, whatever you are feeling, however you are feeling, you can connect with that person on a very intimate level, like almost close to God in some way, because they accept you just the way you are. You can express how you're feeling, and you know you are not being judged in any way. It is a very spiritual connection.

When I think about religion and spirituality, I think of God. Building a relationship with God means making that connection, taking time to pray and meditate. It means trusting in God with all my heart and all my soul. To have faith that in spite of everything that is going on, it is going to be okay. It is about learning more about the word and allowing the word not from the perspective of man's point of view but seeking out my own truth. To define what the truth is for me. I had to go through a lot of transitions just seeking out what the truth is for me, and that can change and that is okay.

When I think about what is just, it is about treating people the way you want to be treated. However, what is "fair" is a tough thing, because we always say, "Oh, that just isn't fair." Your mom says you can go to the movies but then says you cannot go, and you say, "Oh, that is just not fair." But you never know the real reasons why the decisions were made. Thinking about what is fair is kind of tough, but if I just think about it, just off the cuff, I would say it is being respectful and not limiting others because of your own narrow thinking. It is about allowing and being open to seeing someone else's perspective and being courageous enough to take chances and not to be afraid. I think that is part of being fair.

In regard to cultural sensitivity, stop to think about the decisions you make before you act on them. If you want to be culturally sensitive and be diverse, be accepting of others. Stop and take a look at someone who is different from you and get to know them before you make a decision about them as an individual. Stop and look at that; take the courage and give yourself your own opportunity because your own life will be enriched for it. There is so much that others from different races and backgrounds have to offer you. You spend time with children, and you know they are so much different from us. They have so much to offer; well, so do other races. Get away from thinking that your culture is better than someone else's culture; don't have a feeling that someone else is superior or that someone else is inferior. We all put our clothes on the same way, and we all sit on the toilet in the same way. You may have more than someone else, but you are no better; we all have the same feelings. Look at it. Just think, if you deal with depression, you pretty much have the same feelings of depression, anger, and hurt. Well, think about someone else: that human being is just like you. You are just a mirror. Some human beings may be tall, some may be short, some may be thin, or some may be fat, but you are just another image of yourself—you are all the same. So if you take the time to learn about someone else whose culture is different from yours, that may be the best thing you ever learn.

"It's so clear that you have to cherish everyone.
I think that's what I get from these older black women,
that every soul is to be cherished, that every flower is to bloom."
—Alice Walker

Brainy Quote.
http://www.brainyquote.com/quotes/authors/a/alice_walker/2.html.
Accessed December 22, 2010.

INTRODUCING SOUL SISTER
LORNA HOLMES-JACOBSON

IN THE YEAR 2000, MUCH was changing for me. I had been promoted several times with very good salary increases. It was time to have a plan of action to retire, and I was beginning to see light at the end of the tunnel. I had a plan to retire within the next five to six years. My marriage to Jean-Pierre was good and stable. We had been married long enough to go through all the trials and tribulations of raising a blended family and dealing with ex-spouses who could not adjust, and we had even been separated for two years but found ourselves again back in each other's arms. We made a commitment to each other, and we began a new chapter in our marriage and our life together. With our children grown and married, we had added to our family circle several new family members, such as daughters-in-law, sons-in-law, and many beautiful grandchildren. We enjoyed traveling and every few years visiting family friends in Europe. We were financially stable after many years of struggling and counting our pennies. We owned four pieces of property. We were landlords, with the ups and downs of that adventure, and we had plans to build our own home and pay off our bills. Things were finally looking up.

It was during this time that I met Lorna. The first day I met Lorna, I knew I would like her. She had this warmness about her even when she was not smiling. Her features were round, and she took very good care of herself in makeup, hairdos, and outfits. She was smart from the start, but I also knew there was something special about her. She reminded me of someone I might have known from my childhood or old neighborhood when I was a kid. It did not take long before we started getting to know each other better. I was now working in the North East Bay service area of Kaiser Permanente as a service director in human resources. She had come in to be an assistant to one of the lead people in quality. We had a great team of people working in human resources, and I really felt Lorna was good for the department. She

96

was intelligent and a quick learner to our health care system and operations. She enjoyed laughing and making light fun of sometimes challenging issues. I always felt that whenever we were to work together on a project, she would put her whole self into the project and give it her best.

Lorna is the type of person you would just love to go to lunch with. She is so easy to talk to, and somehow you know what you both share at that table will be kept confidential. So you feel completely at ease to be yourself around her. Lorna and I secured our friendship. I was invited to her wedding to share in the celebration of her special day. Soon after that, she moved just a few blocks away from me in Vacaville, California. I was glad for that because by then Lorna and I had really begun to know each other. I had left our home in Cool, California. We rented it out, and I relocated to Vacaville, California, so I would be closer to my new service area at work. I lived in a beautiful house in Vacaville, with a wonderful landscaped yard that had a hot tub and swimming pool. All I could think about was that when work was stressful, I could come home and take a dip in the pool during the hot summer months.

It was at this time that Lorna invited me to her house in Vacaville for a family party. I was glad that she had included me to come see her new home. When I arrived, I found Lorna pretty busy making the food preparations. She was frying stuffed mushrooms, and as she was about to transfer the mushrooms from the frying pan to the large serving tray, I asked her if she would like my help. I said, "Let me arrange them in a straight line for you." She said to me quickly, "Well, that is not needed because I'm going to show you how a black woman does it!" With that said, she immediately dumped all the mushrooms on the platter into a big heap, and then she said to me, "See there? That's how I do it." We both shared in the laughter of a difficult moment made light by Lorna.

Several months passed before our relationship and trust would really be put to the test. I was asked by leadership to come into Lorna's department as a change agent and to identify problem issues and concerns about customer service and employee performance and behavioral issues. It worried me because I could not say no to leadership, but I was concerned about how this would affect my personal relationship with Lorna. I was just hoping that our relationship was strong enough for her to trust me. I decided to meet with Lorna to discuss what I was asked to do and to let her know I would be in her department for a few days to discuss some things leadership wanted to know. I also let her know that I would share with her first about my discoveries and recommendations for improving the customer service issues and the employees' job performance and behavioral issues. She seemed to be fine with the process and glad that I shared with her my thoughts and feelings. I was being completely honest with her; I knew that would be the only way to keep our personal and professional relationship solid. I also knew the true test of our relationship would be when I actually stayed in her department for several days for the discovery process.

I can say Lorna was true to her word and never made me feel like I was infringing on her, her department, or her staff. She put trust in the process, and I was really grateful for that. I believe she knew in her heart that I had nothing to do with this assignment and that it was just an assignment I was given to perform. Lorna never once made me feel bad or let the process come between us. I felt this placed Lorna a step above others who would let something like this affect their friendship. This was a true sign to me of our lasting friendship and that it was important to both of us not to jeopardize what we each valued—our respect for each other. Since that time, Lorna and I have stayed connected by trusting the process of true soul sister relationships.

With every soul sister, writing this book has proven over and over again the importance of listening to understand each other and discover the wisdom and knowledge we each hold. Their sharing of their life stories helps us all better understand each other. Lorna is my soul sister because we have the ability not only to respect each other, but we have accomplished the great feat of trusting each other. Trust is a level one reaches after achieving a respectful relationship. It is higher than respect because it means there is no judgment or withholding, that when you speak the truth, somehow the other person knows it is the truth. Trust is the essence of building a wonderfully solid relationship that will sustain a lifetime. Here is Lorna's story.

"I'll Show You How a Black Woman Does It!"
by Lorna Holmes-Jacobson

Lorna Phyllise Holmes-Jacobson, that is. Actually my grandmother's first name is Phyllis, but my mother did not think Lorna Phyllis sounded good so she spelled it as Phyllise, with an *e* at the end, and changed the pronunciation.

I was born in Berkeley, California, July 14, 1962. I lived there until I was about one and a half, and then our house burned down and we lost everything. Our next-door neighbors had two kids. They were older than I, and they had been told not to play with matches. They went into the closet and played with matches, and our houses were made of shingle roofs and the houses were so close together that the kids died in the fire. I must have been two or something because I still remember my parents picking me up out of bed; we had a one-bedroom house, and it had a big family room out of which they made a bedroom for my sister and me. The living room was in a walk-through in the house, and the kitchen was off to the side. The house next to us that caught fire was right next to my and my sister's bedroom. We were in cribs, and I remember being snatched up and my parents running out of the bedroom door. That is all I can remember of that event. I was the youngest daughter at that time. The house was on Kain Street in Berkeley.

Then we went to live with my mother's older sister Dierdre; she actually lived kind of around the corner from where we were living in Berkeley. She opened her house to us; there was me, my mom, my dad, and my sister, and we all joined her and her three children. It was a tight squeeze, but we stayed for about a year and a half until we got enough money together to put a down payment on another house. We got a house in Richmond in 1965, where I started kindergarten at Stege Elementary School. It was not a great neighborhood, but at the time it was good for what we wanted to do.

My mother went to UC Berkeley; she was a teacher, with a degree in US history. In Richmond she taught in Nystrom School, which was in a very bad neighborhood on South Tenth Street. They considered it a project school; most of the kids' parents were on drugs, and it was just a real scary situation. My mother has gone up and down the scale of different levels of teaching but she mostly taught in elementary schools. She taught third grade for a long time, and then she switched over to first grade at Riverside Elementary School until she retired.

My dad worked in the post office, and before that he worked at the railroad yards in Oakland, California. He went back to school and got a degree at CA State Hayward in kinesiology and physiology. He stayed with the post office, but he did do some substitute teaching at one time.

My father was originally from Monroe, Louisiana. It is a very swampy, woodsy-type area of the country. My mother was from Franklin, Louisiana, which is outside of New Orleans. I saw this picture once of my mother and my Uncle David; my mother was a baby on a little bench outside of a little wood shanty house with a dirt floor that was their home.

My mother was a quarter white, since my great-grandfather was white. My grandmother has Choctaw Indian, French, and African American in her. A lot of my mother's side of the family are very fair and have red hair and gray eyes. I have cousins right now who look like that; you would not know they are black if they didn't tell you, but they are my first cousins.

My grandmother was the daughter of a slave, and she had an eighth-grade education. When she finished school, she taught school for a while, and it was her dreams to have all her four children go to college. My Uncle Aimes was the youngest son, and he died in the Vietnam War. I believe that after he died, they bought this house in East Oakland with the money they got from the military, and that's where my mother grew up.

I remember my mother told me that when they first came here from Louisiana after the war, they lived in the projects in West Oakland; the kids slept in beds, but they did not have much of anything else. The floors were dirt, and they put four in the bed together, with each child facing the opposite direction. In other words, one child's head would be at the top of the bed, and the next child's head would be at the bottom.

My grandmother worked on the military base, and my grandfather worked at the Oakland army base. Whenever they had money, she would come home with a chicken; that chicken had to feed six people, and she used to cook a lot of gravies. It is amazing what my grandmother could do with just one chicken. My grandmother would go down to the market and buy just two pieces of meat, and then she would come home and feed all of us—my grandparents, my mother, my father, my sister, and me. It would feed all of us because she made gravy as well as rice and vegetables. She really knew how to stretch out a meal.

Now with my father, we never had to worry about stretching a meal; at our home, you got your own steak. So it was really strange for me when I went to visit my grandmother; with my brothers and my sisters over there, I would see how she would do things. Afterward I would listen to my mother tell how she had to stretch everything she had. She was really an amazing woman.

My dad is a little different. My father grew up mostly with just his mother. I do not know what the story is because they cover it up, but my grandmother was married to his father for a short period of time, and he was from that first marriage. So all my uncles and aunts on that side are half-sisters and half-brothers, and they are the ones I grew up knowing. I used to wonder why Grandma's name was Lovette and my father's was Holmes. He would say it was Holmes but because she got married again, now it is Lovette. I always wanted the last name Lovette because I thought it was a great name; since it is a French name, it sounded better to me than Holmes. My grandmother (on my mother's side) had four kids, and my mother was the baby in her family. My grandmother on my dad's side was a shipyard builder; she supported her whole family by working in the Oakland shipyards when they came here during the war. I'm not quite sure what my grandfather did; I think not much of anything except drink and gamble. There were five kids there, and my father practically raised all his brothers and sisters while my grandmother worked.

My paternal grandmother was a housekeeper and did odd jobs, and she finally hooked up with this really wealthy sea captain who lived in the Kensington Hills. She would go every day and take care of him and his wife, and that was her thing.

I grew up mostly in Richmond. For the first couple of years, I went to Stege Elementary School, which was predominantly a black school. The schools were not zoned at that time, and my mother thought we would just go there. School was not a challenge for me because I was extremely intelligent; what they used to do when I was in first grade was they would take me out of class and place me in the third-grade class reading block. The kids hated me because I had eczema and I looked different from them. My mother always kept my hair in pretty ribbons and barrettes, and I had long hair that I would sit on when I was younger. The kids hated my hair because typically African Americans do not have hair like that; I was teased and bullied.

A lot of kids used to kick me and pull my hair and call me ratchet girl. They would spit on me and would not be my friends just because I looked different from them. I never understand it because one of those bully kids lived on my block. We lived in the same model house, and she had brothers and sisters just like me. My mother got tired of it and at one point transferred us to Madera Elementary School in the El Cerrito area. This was when the busing program came into play in the 1960s. There were issues that the black children in schools were not getting the same exposures and challenges as others. It may have started in the South, but it also came here, which a lot of people do not know. So they started to integrate the schools here as well. We were getting on the yellow school bus every morning by 7:30 to 7:45 a.m., so we had to get up at seven o'clock. I remember in my class there were not very many black kids and now everyone was just as smart as I was. That made me work harder, and it was actually better for me because it was easier for me to communicate with the kids there because they were as smart as me.

I was very jealous of those children because I was coming from the flatlands to go up on the hill. Way up on top of the hill at Arlington Boulevard, they had these huge monster homes, and these children were coming from families of doctors and lawyers; you could see how big the houses were. As you would go up the hill, the houses would get bigger, with grander pillars in front, bricks, and pool houses. I always wondered what it would be like to live in one of those houses. I would imagine it from the seat of the yellow school bus. I asked my parents why we did not live that way, and my parents said, "We are doing the best we can for you. We may not be able to afford that lifestyle for you, but at least we can afford you the same education they are getting so in time you can go out and get it yourself."

My biggest value and belief when I was a child was to treat everyone the way I wanted to be treated. I learned not to judge people on sight. The reason I say that is because my best friend was a Mormon, and I met her at that school; she had blonde hair and blue eyes, and she was my best friend. Her father was a lawyer, and they raised rabbits and ducks and made their own bread. They had five children, and they lived in this huge house. It was always an experience to go there and visit with her. Her name was Andrea Layton, and I went to church with her too.

My father would say he never wanted me to say that the reason I did not accomplish something was because I was black—that had to be the last reason. He would say that would have to be the last reason to use; if there was nothing else, that had to be it. So professionally I always try to ask myself if I have done something that was not to the best of my ability, was I not competent in what I did? That's before I think of anything else. I am still true to those values today; I do not judge, and that is how I raise my children today. They do not see in color.

When I think about what is just or fair, unfortunately because we live in America, nothing is fair. "Just" to me is everyone having an equal start, having access to the same things in life, and just giving everyone a fair chance. It is not that way. I think being a minority makes it a little different for us, and I think we have to decide what we are going to accept as just. There are things that have happened in my life that made me think, "Well, Lorna, you know it is not fair because the world is not fair." So instead of complaining about unfairness, you should be thinking about what you are going to do about it to make it better for yourself. I been taught this way, so I guess in terms of what is just, I guess you have to determine that for yourself.

My family is most important to me because friends come and go but family is always going to be there. You can love them or hate them, but they are going to be there all your lives whether you want them or not. I do not need a lot of materialistic things in life. I'm just happy being around the people I care about and spending time with them. That to me is the whole purpose of living.

My personal opinion is I think people can do whatever they want to do. I do not think people should put limits on themselves; and the older I get, the more I understand how true that is. Working these last ten years at my most recent employer, I got brainless. I was thinking they were the only employer for me. I failed to look outside the box to see that there were other opportunities for me, so in leaving it has been very difficult for me to let go. I made a decision to step down because the company did not appreciate the value of the ideas that I brought to the table. I felt so strongly about this, that it became an issue of what was more important to me—sticking to my guns, or conceding defeat and complying with the norm or the company's ideas. I felt that it was more important to hold my ground and recognize my individuality and originality were worth far more than keeping a job, so I made a decision to walk away from the company, and that's why I left.

When you close one door, another one opens. I often think about something my grandmother said: "Never stop learning because when you stop learning you die." So, I thought, *Here is a great opportunity for me to do all the things I always wanted to do in life.* I had been weighed down with my employer to do other things in my life.

So now I'm doing things I want to do for myself. I'm learning about insurance, which I would never have considered. I went to a presentation, and I was so mesmerized by the insurance business. Every day when I go to the mailbox, these insurance companies are writing saying, "Come work for me." Then there is like at least ten e-mails a day saying, "You would be great at this," so I thought maybe I would be.

Mentoring has always been my passion, to bring out the good in people and to have them believe in themselves. When mentoring, you really have to look deep within someone. They have to look deep within themselves. Just because they cannot see does not mean it is not there. I think the experience of bringing it out and then getting personal satisfaction that you helped that person achieve whatever they wanted to achieve is the ultimate reward, and that is why I'm passionate about mentoring.

To me, money means comfort. I do not think I will ever have enough money, but I think we will get by and it is not the most important thing to me. When I left the medical center I worked for, my husband, Rhys, said to me, "What are we going to do when we do not have your income?" I said, "We are going to do what we do best. We are going to figure it out." So here we are without an income from me and we are living on my disability, and somehow or another we manage to make it work. It is not comfortable all the time, but we still have our house, our cars, and food on the table. We actually took a vacation. So now we have to decide when I am going to tell them that I formally quit so I can begin a new career. I'm going to take my 401 money and fix things that need to be done in the house. I do know money is just not a huge thing to me; I have everything I need now for me and my family.

To me, happiness is freedom and peace of mind, like being there for when my kids need me and being able to go on vacation when I want to. I just pretty much feel like I'm a free spirit and I can do pretty much what I want; I do not feel weighed down like I felt before, with all the stress of the world on my shoulders for years.

The word "soul" means a lot of different things to me. It means spirituality, it means something from the heart, it is something you can feel, and it is part of what makes us human. When I think of "soul," I think of my own soul and how I talk to my mom. Even though she is gone, she is still very much a part of my life. I feel her presence all the time. When I'm doing something that my grandmother has advised me on, one of the things she said was, "You are really smart." When I started to do this insurance stuff, I could hear her say, "Yes, that's what you need to do." So I know she is there egging me on.

A soul sister to me means someone who has the same spiritual connection you have, who feels things on a spiritual level. Like you know when I'm thinking about Susan, and we do make those connections. Sometimes I may not pick up the phone to call her, but when I do, it may be two days later because she is on my mind. I do not know why we do this, but I believe we have a spiritual connection that way between us. When you sit in the room with soul sisters, you can feel that.

Susan wanted me to give an example of how a black woman does it. Well, just yesterday my car window was broken, and I was pissed off because the repair was going to be over three hundred dollars because it is not covered by the warranty. It has been broken five times; it's always the same piece, and the window will not stay up. I had to go to the car dealership, and I had to act like a black woman. What I mean by that is I'm not going to pay for it. I had made up my mind that I was not going to pay for it for the fifth time. They were going to have to make a deal with me to get me out of their dealership. To get me to shut the hell up, this repair was going to get done on their dollar. After I explained to them how it was going to happen, guess what? It happened; I did not pay a dime. To me that is how a black woman does it. If you've got to get something done, you are not going to pull any punches. I could go in there and talk to them reasonably, but I know that is not going to work. So I've got to get loud, I've got to put my hand on my hip, and I've got to cock my head to the side. I've got to give them some attitude so I can get some action.

When I do not act this way, I get the runaround. Another example: Rhys tried to talk to our refinance company about our house. They gave him the runaround, and he was really pissed off. I said, "Oh no, give me that phone number." I called and said, "This is what we are going to do, and this is how we are going to do it." We got everything we wanted. We got the refinance. They had a cookie-cutter process for how they deal with borrowers, but I convinced them that rules were negotiable and that we could meet their terms, if they would be flexible with us. This is what we did, and because I was able to convince them, they negotiated successfully with us. Typically they do not accept payments, and they wanted a lump sum for the payment. I said, "We only have this much money, so this is what we are going to do. We are going to pay you four hundred dollars today, eight hundred dollars in two weeks, and three hundred dollars later." I laid out a payment plan for them, and they said, "Okay." You know it had to get done because we were going to lose the house.

When I get under pressure and something needs to get done and it is not happening, Rhys will say, "I need you to be a black woman and take care of this." I know what that means: the hands go on the hips, I'll make the call, and Lorna is going to put on the red nose and the white pancake makeup and be Bozo the Clown. Whatever the goal is, it is going to get done when I do that. There you have it. One more thing on this, I think it is the intimidation factor since a lot of people who are not black and even some black people cannot handle a black with that level of determination and that kind of tenacity. I think it came from women in my family being told they could not do something. I know it comes from me when people tell me I cannot do something. That is like writing me a ticket to do it. Yes, you push me up against a wall, and I will say, "I can do it."

In my culture, there is this African American saying, "It takes a village to raise a child." I really believe that, and it does not have to be family, just a community you live in. I think I am a very accepting person, so if your children come over to my house, you have left them in my care and they become my kids. If I would do this for my own children, I will do it for your kids too. I believe there is a strong sense of community, and I would trust that the parent would trust me to do just that. Again, that goes back to treating others the way you want to be treated yourself.

I guess in my culture, we all have similar beliefs about community service. My family used to have two reunions a year. It was fun because all my aunts and uncles would come on over, and everybody was expecting to see my crazy

Aunt Leila or my Aunt Candi. You cannot have it without my Uncle "K" coming over and Uncle Doug.

My dad's younger brother Doug was like my protector. My father always described him as not being quite right in the head. He was like the Arnold—the governor of California—of the family due to his size and strength. Uncle Doug was six foot four and very muscular, but he was a teddy bear. He used to be a bus driver for AC transit. When he used to stand up in the bus, his head would touch the ceiling; he would tell the kids to "pipe down," and the kids would shut up. He was a great cook and made the best barbeque pork ribs and chicken. He was really funny. He would take the barbeque paintbrush and say he was making "Michelangelo's" ribs and would paint the ribs.

He taught me how to shoot a gun. He would take two bullets and come back with two ducks; or if he was going rabbit hunting, he would take four bullets and come back with four rabbits. He used to go with his friends hunting. When I was a kid, he was like a jungle gym; we used to swing on his arms. He had these giant muscles and he would hold his arms out, and my sister and I would swing on his arms. He was like a giant kid to us. I remember he would sit on the sofa and shoot at the wood box. He would shoot out the words "wood box." I asked him, "How do you do that?" and so he showed me. We went out one night, and he had a can of butane, a gun, and a flashlight. He would go out to a tree, find a spider, spray it with butane and freeze it, and then shoot it—and the damn thing would drop out of the tree. Do not ask me why, but that is what he did as a pastime.

The family reunion I remember the most was at the Veterans Memorial in Piedmont, California. We had family from Chicago, Texas, and Richmond, and we were all there. We had to have the family talent show. We dressed up in garbage bags like the California raisins. We put on big house shoes and placed buttons on them; my sister played the piano, my cousin Mina played the bass, and we danced to "Boogie-Oogie-Oogie." Then my mother played the piano. At the end of the talent show, we all sang Dionne Warwick's song "That's What Friends Are For." My grandmother was like the family matriarch; she started the talent show off, and when the show was over, my grandmother would come on stage and that was the grand finale.

The food was organized by my grandmother. My father's mother was a very talented part-time caterer, and my Aunt Dierdre still does it out of her house. The way my family does it is they want to know how many people there will be and then they decide on the menu. The food was not a problem because my aunt can take twenty dollars, come out of a store, and feed fifty people and have leftovers. The problem with our family is we like to drink, so we were wondering how we could cover the costs of the alcohol. One family member said, "I know someone, if you have twenty dollars, we can get the alcohol for the family reunion. I do not know where it comes from or anything like that, but just give me a twenty-dollar bill and I will supply everything." She did. It was hysterical. She was talking about going down to Lucky's, and back in those times, they had a big yellow section of generic brands, including generic vodkas. My family is so ghetto, they went and bought all this stuff up and then they got all these fancy decanters, put the alcohol in them, and set them up on the bar. No one knew the difference, and all this champagne came from the outlet. You do not know where all this stuff came from; all you know is your glass is full and it is staying full. So that is how we did it.

We had prime rib, rosemary chicken, fruit plates, and meat trays. We all paid a little bit, ten or twelve dollars for each person. We had at least 110 people. We filled that hall in Piedmont. Then they read the family history. On my father's side of the family, we were related to John C. Calhoun; he was a statesman or Senator, and he was known for his cold blue eyes. If you look at my family's pictures, every couple of generations, someone will pop up with these cold blue eyes. My grandmother had them, but she is a little darker than me. My cousin Cameron has them too, so it is a recessive gene, but because of this family tree, some of the family members have blue eyes.

As for my education, I'm actually twelve units short of a master's degree in education. I have a bachelor of arts degree in English, literature, and liberal arts. I have a postgraduate partnership degree in teacher education. I went to Cal State Hayward, Holy Names, a little time at UC Berkeley, but I finished up in Holy Names in Oakland, California. My biggest joy is learning and reading.

My religion is both Methodist and Baptist, depending on where I'm living. My father's family was Baptist, so when we were with my grandmother, we were Baptist. My grandmother on my mother's side is Methodist. The difference between the two is the Methodists tend to be more reserved in the way they worship. In the Baptist church, the people would fall off the pews if the music got real good and they got excited. They were very loud, and they used to have nurses run down the aisle with fans to catch the people who were falling out. It was like a sideshow. It was just the way they feel; it is a different expression of how they believe. I know in the Methodist church, they would carry on too in the church. Mostly it happens during the music, but if the minister's sermon is really moving and he gets the church congregation involved, they will fall out. The term "falling out" is an African American term for people becoming so emotional during a spiritual experience that they physically bend over and fan themselves. Sometimes, they do faint, but often times they become emotionally excited and fall backwards into the pews because the "spirit" overtakes them and makes them physically weak.

In choosing whom I wanted to be with as a life partner, color was never an issue to me. I looked for the man who treated me right. What I mean by that is that I looked for a man who was supportive of me, believed in me, loved me beyond what I look like physically, and could also accept my children as his own.

I'm very blessed that my husband Rhys is all of those things. He might not be perfect, but then, neither am I. Rhys supports the choices I make in life, and he is like the piece of me that is missing. Sometimes I think that I can't do something, and he's right there to say, "Oh, yes, you can do it! And you'll be great too!" Rhys is the kind of man who believes in you even when you are at a point where you've lost faith in yourself. (I've learned this over the past year.) He continues to stand by me and hold me up, even when I don't think I have the strength to do something.

I consider myself a very strong-willed black woman. Sometimes I think it's intimidating to others. When I say others, I mean black men in particular. Not all of them are like that, but it is really difficult to find a black man who doesn't feel threatened by my intelligence. Rhys has never had an issue with that. Mind you, he isn't college-educated or professional in the sense that I am, but he is one of the most intelligent men I have ever known.

Rhys has a steel trap for a mind. He knows geography cold. He knows about electrical wiring, he can build computers from scratch, he can fix cars, and he is a whiz at world history. It is very easy for me to have an intelligent conversation with him, even on abstract subjects that would lose most people. He is not afraid to challenge my opinion, nor is he intimidated by my level of intelligence.

Honestly, being married to Rhys is like being on a great date that never ends. We have extremely different tastes when it comes to music, but because of our ability to accept the cultural differences of what the other likes, we are open to listening to different types of music. For example, I hate heavy metal, and Rhys hates R&B and rap music, but we both like rock, folk, classical, reggae, and easy listening music. He is often surprised when he plays some of his music that I start to sing along. We both have a passion for the Beatles, which is something he didn't know when he met me. Both of us enjoy strategic games like chess, Clue, or Monopoly. We also both enjoy poker.

I think the only people who notice Rhys is white and I am black and that we are married are people outside of our relationship. I know that on numerous occasions when we go to the grocery store together, the clerk looks at us and asks, "Are you together?" I've gone to restaurants with my husband, and the maitre d' has asked each of us if we're dining alone.

I feel the "looks" we get when we go out sometimes. It really seems to bother everybody else, instead of us. When I look at my husband, I don't see a white man. I see the man I fell in love with. I see a man with a huge heart and great family values, who is a pillar of strength. He is a good man, because he looks beyond all of my flaws (of which there are a great many) and he accepts me just as I am.

I guess in the grand scheme of things, color doesn't really matter unless you're talking about the color of the heart, and that is definitely red!

Ain't I a Woman?

That man over there says that women need to be helped into carriages, and lifted over ditches, and to have the best place everywhere. Nobody ever helps me into carriages, or over mud-puddles, or gives me any best place! And ain't I a woman?

Look at me! Look at my arm! I have ploughed and planted, and gathered into barns, and no man could lead me! And ain't I a woman?

I have borne thirteen children, and seen most all sold off to slavery, and when I cried out with my mother's grief, none but Jesus heard me! And ain't I a woman?

Sojourner Truth (1797–1883)
Canfield, et al., *Chicken Soup for the African American Soul (Deerfield Beach, Florida:* Health Communications, Inc., 2004), 8.

INTRODUCING SOUL SISTER DONELL ALLEN

I MET DONELL ALLEN WHEN I first transferred from South Sacramento to the Diablo service area. I was hired as a change agent with a one-year assignment to turn around a very unruly clerical department. If I could accomplish this task, I would be promoted again, with additional assignments and more wage increases. I'm happy to say I was successful in this task and was beginning to get a name for myself by developing a successful track record of building teams and developing leadership qualities in others.

Donell Allen was someone I did not know, but I felt drawn to her. She was working in administration in Walnut Creek Medical Center when I first met her. She, too, was friendly, competent, and intelligent, and I felt very confident just by the way she carried herself. She likes to talk and was friendly to me. Not knowing anyone at the time, I felt this was a great start for me. I would often go into administration to meet with the leadership, and Donell was there as an administrative assistant. She was always kind and had a welcoming smile to match. I did not know at that time that there was a plan in store for us that would open many doors of getting to know each other better, and that this friendship would blossom into a lifetime of knowing and caring about each other.

We next came together at a diversity training class. We were working together on assignments and discovered through the process that our personality types were similar on how we processed information. I learned that Donell was the type of person that prefers to make a connection with you on a personal level before going straight to the issue of problem solving. For example, she responds well to, "How are you?" and "How are things going with you and your family?" We joked about this several times after the learning class. When we would meet in the hallways, it seemed to open up our friendship to another level.

After a few years, Donell and I came to work together after she received

111

her college degree in human development from Cal State Hayward, which is now called Cal State East Bay. She was promoted into the same department as I was in 2005. It was my last year of employment before retiring. Our job was to open a new department in quality assurance and to help change and improve the existing program with an electronic software program. Donell was a whiz and very capable of doing many things at a high level of delivery. I admired her and her ability to work with a leader who was very trying at times, being overly obsessed with micromanaging us and everything else.

The human resources leader knew it was my last year of employment and asked if I would mentor Donell for a management position. It was hoped that she would replace me. It was at this time I got to really learn more about Donell as a person. My mission was to prepare her for management, get her ready to manage a staff, and basically take over since I was nearing retirement within the next six months. During this time, I found Donell to be open to learning, and she was a quick learner. She had many talents and skills. She was multitalented and could perform many tasks at a high level. She was definitely a high achiever and took pride in her accomplishments. When she laughed, she laughed with her whole heart in an open and carefree manner, much like I had done so many years ago.

As we grew closer with our work experience, I learned some things about her personal life. She was going through a painful, surprising divorce. It had an earth-shattering effect on her. Having been down that road twice, I tried to offer some worldly advice, but little seemed to comfort her during this painful period. I guess in many cases like this, one just has to go through the process themselves to discover the freedom it comes with. She was not ready to accept it, and it had all come as a huge shock to her. At the same time, she was committed to her job and the assignments of learning about management and how to manage others with human resource skills of caring and understanding.

It was through this learning of getting to know her more and understanding who she was that I grew to love and care about Donell. She was the person I had been many years earlier, and I needed to help her understand that she was going to make it in this world, even if it had to be done on her own.

In any event, I cannot to this day say how much Donell reminds me of my old self. As I learned more about her painful childhood experiences, I could not help but compare my life to hers. We had lived similar childhoods within the family unit. Our childhoods were all about secrets and not telling anyone what was going on in your house. We shared all the disappointments of family life, the lack of family trust and respect, and the physical, mental, and emotional abuse that comes with having dysfunctional parents. Growing up in a state of fear does something to you. The only way out of the spiral of despair is to face your demons. I know because I was there once in my life. Donell, like me, has managed to reclaim her life and live a life of complete freedom after growing up in a living hell. It is because of these similarities that we have shared in life that I have selected Donell as my soul sister. Here is her dynamite life story.

"A Leap of Faith with a Winning Heart"
by Donell Allen

LIFE IS GOOD. LIFE IS full of surprises. Life is full of adventure, and opportunities abound. Life is what you make of it. A question ... How can a person believe in this? How can a person think life is good or adventurous when it is full of experiences that hurt? How can a person think that life has opportunities available to everyone when all you can see is bars on the windows of your house when you look outside and all you can hear is gunfire at night and helicopters flying overhead in the evening shining spotlights over your neighborhood searching for someone? If you are of another color or do not belong to a gang, nightfall can be very dangerous. People are consistent in their inconsistencies. People wear masks to hide who and what they are to others. How can a person know who is truthful and who is deceiving? How can a person believe there is something beautiful in life when all they can see is the darkness? How can a person trust others when most wear invisible masks? It is called taking a leap of faith, believing in something before it can be seen.

My Origins

I was born in Richmond, California. I am Italian, French, and German. I was raised in an Italian family setting in the heart of Richmond. My father did not graduate from high school; he was a truck driver. My father had black hair, brown eyes, and olive skin, and he was of average height. He reminded me of Fred Flintstone, but most women thought he was very handsome. My mother graduated from high school and did clerical jobs before I was born. She continued to work until I was three years of age. I am the oldest of three children; my brother and sister are fraternal twins. My sister received a diagnosis of a rare heart condition at the age of eight months. She almost died three times before the age of two. My brother and I were cast aside; we were the healthy children and, therefore, we did not need attention, according to our parents. At the age of eight, in a way, I took on my brother as my own child. We provided companionship to each other that we did not receive from our parents. It could be said that my brother and I are more like twins than he and my sister.

I lived in an apartment for the first eight years of my life. We were poor, but I was not aware of it at the time. My father was abusive—verbally, spiritually, and physically. From the time I was born, I did not like him. He reminded me, many times, that as a baby, I would not let him hold me. I would scream every time I was in his arms. Could it be that I felt unsafe with him even as an infant? Because of the anger and meanness that oozed out of him, I thought he was the most hideous person alive. I just did not see what others saw. Perhaps it was because he did not treat them the way he did those he loved.

My mother loved and cherished him. Why? I will never know, but she did. I learned later on that no one on my mother's side liked my father. They only tolerated him. But wait, this is about me. Why am I writing about my father? He did help shape me into who I am today, so I should be thankful and I am. But I am also hurt that he never showed or expressed love and acceptance of me.

When I was growing up, he ignored me except when he was drunk and needed something or berated me for something I could have or could not have done. The messages I received from my father were: "You grow up. You do not need a college education as you are not worth it and we are not paying for it. You will grow up, find a nice Italian boy, get married, have children, and he will take care of you because you are not capable of caring for yourself. You are stupid, ugly, fat, and worthless. You are like most women. Don't cry because I do not want to hear your pain or your hurt. Don't laugh too much or too loud because your voice is annoying. Children should be seen and not heard. Do not ever do anything that will make your family, especially me, look bad. Do not ever complain to anyone because what happens in this family stays in this family. If you do tell anyone, I will do terrible things to you. I will hit you, slap you, and mentally beat you down. And if that does not work, I will start in on your mother and your brother."

Remember that my father never said any of these things to me. However, now that I am older, educated, and out of psychotherapy, I have some vocabulary to articulate his nonverbal communications.

My mother? I loved my mother and felt sorry for her as well. When I was growing up, my mother cared for me and showed me love. But my mother was a distant woman and was also busy caring for my father, whom she loved. I think she was afraid he would leave her and then she would be alone. My mother was always quick to laugh, had a fun sense of humor, and was adventurous. She had big green eyes and a wonderful smile, and was petite in stature. She was fair-skinned and had light brownish-blonde hair. She never had a negative thing to say.

My great-grandma, K, lived with us for the first three years of my life. I miss her. She was the one who took care of me and protected me from my parents' fights and my father's drunken rampages. One day she told them she was moving back with my aunt; it was my mother's turn to take on the responsibilities of motherhood, to stay home and raise her daughter. Great-Grandma K left me at the age of three with my parents. My mom had to quit work, and my father could not buy new toys like he could before. They now had to be responsible adults, with a child in tow who was strong-willed, argumentative, and curious. Great-Grandma K never remarried but stayed with her three children until she died in her eighties.

There were three women and one man in my life that I looked up to, and they helped me survive. The matriarchs in my family were Grandma A, Great-Grandma Z, and Great-Grandma K, and then there was my Grandpa M. Almost every weekend, I would go to Grandma A's house and sleep over. I was able to play house and terrorize my Grandpa M's garden. I would help him pull weeds and plant, play in his mulch pit, and eat the vegetables out of his garden. He would take me fishing with him; he taught me how to find my own bait and put my pole together. He told me that I needed to know how to do this in case I found myself in a place where I had no job and had to eat. He taught me to plant a garden, how to fertilize it using leftover food, what to eat, and how to prepare it.

Grandma A taught me how to bake, cook, and clean. For the most part, she loved my grandpa. Grandma A would listen to me as I cried about my dad. She was my confidant. I think that is why she took me on the weekends. She knew that when my father was drunk, he would act out and it was not very safe for me.

Great-Grandma Z was the strongest woman out of my family. She did not need to hide anything. She just told it like it was. My great-grandma came from Sicily; she was bought by my great-grandfather when she was fourteen years old. He was twenty years her senior. She was pretty much a slave, even though he did marry her. After giving birth to two children, she left him. She left one son with him, my Uncle A, and she took the other son, Grandpa M, with her. She took off on her own and I am not sure how she survived, but she remarried my Great-Grandpa Z and had three more children with him.

At my great-grandparents' house, I learned how to raise snails for eating, how to run a household, and how strong and respected a woman should be. When my dad would get out of hand, my great-grandma would come in and yell at him in Italian. That was the only language she spoke. I understood it as well. She would tell him to sit down and shut up and not talk to or treat me badly. In her house, she was the boss. In her house, I could do what I wanted and be happy. My father would sit down and smile at her and do what she said. I so loved her for that. She died when I was five. I did not know her for long, but I feel like she is always with me.

This was a woman who came from another country, did not speak the language, did not know the customs, was sold to a man whom she had never met, and was expected to accept her lot in life, to believe what other people thought her place was in life and to be happy about it. She took her life and made it what she wanted. It takes courage to leave and walk the path of life on your own, even more when you have a child in tow. She had no money, barely knew the language, had no support from her family, and had no close friends. Yet she made it. And she came out stronger, with a good sense of who she was, an excellent sense of self, and a loving, kind, and caring person.

But my whole family had addiction issues. Wine would be drunk every night—at least a bottle apiece. My mother and grandmother drank whisky throughout the day and took prescription drugs. I learned at a young age that any emotion that was not happy should be extinguished.

This is where my story begins.

As I said, I was born in Richmond—the wrong color and the wrong gender. Here I was an outsider, and there was very little hope for me to aspire to anything better than being a wife to a blue-collared worker—and that was if I was lucky. I am five feet two inches tall, with blonde hair and green eyes. Some would say that I am attractive. I had little or no encouragement from my mother or father to be anything but a wife and a mother. I had no dreams of a higher education, travel, or meeting others different from me. I was encouraged to hide anything negative or unhappy from the world as much as possible. Instead of being encouraged to get out, I was encouraged to hide. "Do not try to be better or different," I was told; this was where I was born, and I was expected to stay and make the most of it. I was expected to rely upon others for my well-being, safety, and decisions. For a while, I believed them. This was all I knew; we did not travel. My father's idea of a vacation was to stay home; a day out on the town would be to take a drive into Berkeley and look at other people. We could only go out to visit the places that were familiar, his parents' home and McDonalds. Everything else was considered unsafe or undesirable. I would always ask to get out of the car so that I could go into the stores or see the vendors on the street, touch their wares, ask questions, and smell the scents of the street. This was not allowed, as those vendors on the street were not Italian—they were dark, different, and not to be trusted.

What I later discovered is that my father was not trustworthy nor did he trust others. He did not think highly of himself; he felt he was less than others because of his education and place in life. His child could not be better than he. I grew to hate him tremendously.

My father taught me many types of things. I learned how to keep a poker face, agree with him, and keep all feelings out of my eyes and heart. If he detected anything, I would have been hit or thrown into a wall. He was teaching me how to survive in the jungle, the one I was born into, the one where the slightest show of fear, softness, empathy, or compassion was considered weakness. These skills came in handy as I made my way through school. I had to take the bus from my home to a better school on the hill. I was in high school. It was those trips to and from school that I had to survive. No show of fear and the knowledge of how to use a knife kept me company on these rides. I was usually vigilant, distrustful of others, and emotionally detached. The times I did let my guard down on these trips, twice, I suffered. Both times, I was beat up, and things were stolen from me. At that point, I told my parents that either they figured out how to get me to and from school or I was not attending. It was their responsibility to ensure that I was safe and received an education; parents owe that to their children. It was not my fault they chose to live in an area that was impoverished, dark, and unsafe. What could they say? I was right. After that, they made sure that I received a ride to and from school minus the bus.

I did not have many friends in my childhood years. I was not allowed to have friends of color, and those that were similar to me lived on the hill. No one from the hill would be caught dead at the house of someone that lived by the tracks. As I grew older, I did have two close friends. One friendship lasted through high school, the other through our mid-twenties. I built friends in the books I read or the movies that I watched. I learned to have an active and creative imagination. I began working at fourteen years of age and had three different jobs by the age of seventeen.

I knew at a young age that I had to move out of my house. There would come a point in time when I would no longer be able to tolerate my father. There was also a longing in me to see what more the world was made of. At the age of nineteen, I took a job in San Francisco at a large paper. That is where I began to explore the world of people, color, boundaries, and myself. I will say that I was terrified of traveling to the city for a job and not sure what was in store for me. This reminded me of the last time I took public transportation, when I was attacked. I was terrified to work in the city and take public transportation as it brought up this type of memory. I was learning what it was like to be female, someone that commanded and received attention in this large city. I found that I liked this; it was very empowering. I was able to get into the clubs at the age of nineteen; they did not look at identification much in those days. Life was fun, good, enjoyable, and full of pleasure and many experiences. I took a leap of faith that things were not always hurtful and that unknown people could be good and kind, just like those in my family.

I began to feel more of a sense of myself. I was defying my father, I was surpassing my father—and I felt empowered. I was better than he. Now that I had a respectable job, it was time to leave home. I bought my first house at the age of nineteen, three blocks away from my parents. My plan was to stay there five years, buy the next house in a better city, and five years after that move again until I ended up in an area that I desired. You see, I did something that my parents did not do until their midlife, and that was to become a homeowner. Not only did I buy a home, but I had a plan for my life. I enrolled in a community college to obtain my degree; I had no idea where I was heading, but I was in school. I had many friends now. I was discovering that the world was not as unsafe as I was led to believe. People who were not Italian were not bad at all. My father was wrong.

At the age of twenty, I was sexually harassed by my boss. I was in shock and had no idea how to handle this except to keep quiet. The old programming from my father came back into play: "Do not bring disgrace to the family," "You deserved it," "Be grateful that you have a job and do nothing to jeopardize it." I left the company months later and never filed charges. Perhaps my father was right—trust no one. However, what perplexed me was that my boss was of European descent. This did not fit what I was taught; my father was wrong yet again.

After that experience, I decided that I did not want to work for others; I wanted to be in charge of myself, my time, my income. I wanted to get out of Richmond; and if I was going to stick with my five-year plan, I needed to make more money than I currently was. At the age of twenty, I went into business for myself, one that would be considered questionable but profitable. However, I realized early on that being in business was not as easy or as profitable as I thought. I was too young and inexperienced to make it work. During this time I met the father of my child. He was Mexican, tall, dark, and handsome. He loved music and dancing and was very exciting. One day we were business associates and the next very close. I blinked my eyes, and he moved in, all within six months. I finally confided in him about the harassment I encountered with my boss. He told me to quit my job because he loved me and would take care of me. I did not love him; however, at the age of twenty-one, coming from where I did, this all sounded like a dream come true, and I bought into the story. Of course, my family did not approve, especially my father. He had very little to do with us and would seldom speak to us. This man was now more attractive to me because my father did not approve. A few months later, he told me he had a vasectomy and that I did not need to take birth control pills. I soon became pregnant. He lied to me. Why? Could it be that my father was right? Oh my God, how could that be?

What to do? I had a really large, ugly secret, and I did not want anyone to know. But in a few months, it would be obvious. I took a leap of faith and told my parents. My mother advised me to do anything I had to but just keep my child. My father told me that I was to keep my child and I had to get married.

After all, that is what any respectable Italian would do. He was very unhappy that the father of my child was not only Mexican, but a very dark Mexican. How could he ever live it down that his eldest daughter was involved with someone not of Italian origin, jobless, pregnant, and not married. I endured many conversations with them yelling, crying, and finally telling me that it was my life and I had to make this decision. It was a dilemma—what to do? I had no job, I was pregnant, and my child's father was not employed. He lied about that as well. I did what any person with my background would do; I went on welfare.

Oh, what a joy. I was dropped off at 6:00 a.m. on a very dark street in the middle of the ghetto to stand in the welfare line to just apply. I was terrified. There was no bus, no metal, no nothing to protect me except the small knife I carried in my purse, now moved to my pocket. I was the only white person in line. I was trying to keep that jungle cat face on so that no one would know just how terrified I was. I was not successful; however, what I found was that instead of being devoured by those folks so unlike me, I was shown support, kindness, and understanding. My own kind left me to fend for myself, and those unlike me were there for me. I cannot say that I formed any lasting friendships that day, but I did find a people, those bonded by misfortune and the will to survive, supporting each other—a village so to speak. My father was wrong again. Another leap of faith; where there appears to be no support, once a step is taken, that path appears. I felt safe with these folks. I felt I belonged with these folks. I felt protective of these folks. This is where I first understood, in my soul, that the outer trimmings of a person are not to be used to judge or know who and what they are about.

I still had to figure out if I should keep my baby, adopt it out, or terminate the pregnancy. After a few weeks, I decided that it was best to terminate. I was in no position to raise a child. I had nothing to offer—no job, no formal education, and I was not sure how long I would be able to keep my house. There seemed to be no logical reason for me to keep my baby. I was going to schedule the procedure the next day. As I was falling asleep, I heard a male voice speaking to me about my baby. He told me that I was to keep my baby and that this baby would save my life—I would have a son. In turn, I was to save his life. What did I do? I actually listened to this male voice. Something I told myself that I would no longer do, listen to what a "father" had to say. I kept my baby; I had a son. There have been many times when we have saved each other through the years.

I did not enjoy being on welfare. This was one of the lowest points in my life. I remember standing in line at the supermarket paying with food stamps. The cashier would roll her eyes at those of us using food stamps, and the customers who had to wait behind while I paid were just as impatient and judgmental. I felt like trash, I felt guilty that I was accepting help from the government, and I knew that I had to get off the system. Looking back, this was a very memorable lesson in humility and resilience.

Six months after my son was born, I knew it was time to terminate the relationship with his father; I could and would make it on my own. I did not have a plan but a strong belief that I could do it—another leap of faith. I would rather live as a single mother than depend upon someone who said one thing but did another. It was not easy; his father threatened to take my son from me, claiming that I was an unfit mother—unfit because I had no income. Let's not forget that I was the one on welfare, and he had no income. He also told me I would never find anyone to take care of me because I was "used goods."

I was on the brink of losing my home, but even though I was on welfare, I was still able to keep the place I lived in since I did not hold a deed—I held a share. However, there was not enough money coming in to pay for everything. I took another leap of faith and asked for help. This time I told my parents that I most likely would have to leave my house and that I was prepared to lose my home and do what I needed to do to ensure that my son and I could survive. My mom provided the help I needed. With her recent inheritance, she paid off the note and then became my bank. I paid her faithfully until the note was repaid with interest. My father did not have a say in what my mother did with her inheritance.

When my son was eleven months old, I went to work at a psychiatric hospital. Looking back, all my jobs came to me. I never had to pound the pavement. Each job that came my way was one for which I was recommended. From the age of fourteen to the present, they have always been more or less handed to me. Looking back, these have been blessings. The jobs that were made available to me have always been more than I thought I was qualified to perform. However, if someone had the foresight to see that I could do the job, then they must see something in me that I did not. This was the beginning of my ability to actually believe that I could do anything that I set my mind to. Never mind the fact that I had survived living in Richmond, buying my first home at the age of nineteen, and not losing it during my first experience of motherhood. I actually could handle being a mother, single at that, and was now ready to enter the workforce again.

I worked at the psychiatric hospital for three years. I started at the bottom and worked my way up to managing the admitting office and learning all the aspects of a business office. In 1990, I came to Kaiser Permanente. My previous boss from the psych hospital, who now worked at Kaiser Permanente, called me one day and said she had three positions, described each one, and asked if I would be interested. Of course, I would have to interview just like the rest of the candidates. I interviewed and selected the job of my choice. I began in a union position, where the job was outlined for you and you did not go beyond your scope. However, I frequently took on other assignments. In one and a half years, I moved to a higher position. In the union, the person with the most seniority is considered for the job regardless of the qualifications. I spent four years working in union positions. I found the union positions unchallenging, and I realized that I wanted more out of life—to be more a part of life and to contribute to the overall good of life. I did not know how to begin to do this, but I knew that I wanted to experience and contribute more; I wanted a career.

I made another close friend, who helped me to remember to believe in myself, that I was intelligent, that all things were possible, and that I needed to complete my formal education. She inspired and challenged me to be better than I could even imagine. My friend was younger than I, a widow at the age of twenty-six. Through her, I learned grace, acceptance, and tolerance. I learned that it is more rewarding to give and to be of service to others than to receive. Our friendship was a huge turning point for changes within me. I thoroughly embraced what it meant to be a parent and how to sacrifice for the greater good of my child, who is part of the future. The sacrifice that I am referring to included the following: 1. Set an example. 2. Place my child's well-being above my own. 3. Strive to reach higher; never settle for less. 4. Take the education I was receiving and put it to use, not only at the company but for the community.

I enrolled in a community college, completed my associate of arts degree, and then went on to obtain my BA in human development. During most of those years, I focused on my son, being a mother, work, and school. In 2002, I graduated with my BA. Going to school opened my eyes to so many more life possibilities. It taught me thinking, seeing, feeling, researching, and not being married to a hypothesis. History and art held a new place in my heart. I fell in love with the conqueror Constantine and dreamed of traveling the Mediterranean to see what he saw. In the study of art, my favorite was Bernini. I have since traveled to France, visited the Louvre, and seen his work "in the flesh." Society shapes who and what we are more than hormones and genes do. Education is fun, and I always want to be learning. To be stagnant is to die. I met so many people going to school and continue to have a close friendship with some.

During this time, I took another leap of faith, and I met the man I married, which lasted four years. I thought I had finally found someone to love, trust, and share my son and my life with. This leap did not work out as I had planned. We were together a total of seven years, during which time, I gained a large and dysfunctional family and two more children. My son finally had a father, siblings, and grandparents—I loved it. I felt as if I was the luckiest person in the world. For a while I was, and then it came to an end. All my skills of planning, communication, analysis, experience, trust, and faith did not prepare me that another person would decide that he no longer wanted to be married. He failed to tell me that he went into the marriage with the concept that if it worked, great—if not, no big deal. Once it began to look like work was needed, that it was no longer fun or easy, he was not interested. What I did not see was that I married someone who just wanted to have fun all the time. He was someone who needed to mask life's realties, such as money and parenting issues. His wife was not always in agreement and would challenge his decisions. What he did not realize was that it ripped our family to shreds. What he did not hear was that I entered the marriage with the belief that we agreed to work as partners, to work through issues, to enjoy both the fun and the not-so-fun aspects of life together. Our definitions of marriage and life partners were vastly different, and neither of us saw that early on.

During some of the most painful events in my life, I moved up from lower positions to one of leadership within this large organization. I had a bachelor's degree, determination, and a huge abyss in my life. By the time my son graduated from high school, I was divorced and had a large void in my life. Taking another leap of faith, I focused on my career and kept the belief in myself that no matter what, I could pull myself out of the abyss that I was falling into. There were many late nights taking on projects that no one else wanted as they were not what one might consider "sexy." I knew I wanted to continue college and obtain my master's degree, but I did not have the ability or desire at this time. Instead, in my forties I became a fitness instructor and now am part owner of a center. I continue my climb up the ladder at the company, positions with more authority and responsibility. I have an impeccable reputation as someone who is going places in the company. I have been approached by those in authority and encouraged to apply for positions with more responsibility, influence, and challenge. In conversations with others in authority, they have complimented me and are impressed with my accomplishments and talent; I have been told that if I want to continue to move up, I must obtain a master's degree. I have conducted informational interviews to ascertain what areas of this organization I would be interested in moving up to.

There have been many times in my career that I have felt that I made a wrong turn or that a path was blocked. When that occurs, I remember my past, the lessons I have learned, experiences I have gained, and the leaps of faith I have taken. Nothing is ever meaningless; each lesson, each person, each hardship I have encountered has provided the necessary education for me to learn and overcome the challenges. Each leap of faith has worked out, perhaps not as I had planned, but in ways that have helped me grow and become wiser. I have finally learned to trust myself, to have the courage to leap when I cannot see. I came from parents who did not believe in themselves; therefore, they were not able to provide me with encouragement, a sense of self, or the confidence that I could be more than I was born into. However, from their lack of support and the environment I was raised in, I developed defiance, a sense of adventure, the ability to give, to trust, to feel safe within myself, to live in the face of adversity—and the ability to leap even if I cannot see where I am going, to trust my instincts.

"You gain strength, courage, and confidence by every experience in which you really stop to look fear in the face. You are able to say to yourself, 'I have lived through this horror. I can take the next thing that comes along.' You must do the thing you think you cannot do."
—Eleanor Roosevelt

"Quotations by Author," Eleanor Roosevelt Quotes—The Quotations Page. Accessed December 22, 2010, http://www.quotationspage. com/quotes/Eleanor_Roosevelt. 1

Introducing Soul Sister Miranda Sanz

I HAVE MANY FOND MEMORIES about Puerto Rico. My husband and I have visited this beautiful country three times while selecting vacation spots. I fell in love with the beauty of old San Juan in Puerto Rico. The San Juan Hotel is one of my favorite places, with beautiful crystal chandeliers in the center of the hotel entrance. One of my favorite times visiting San Juan was an offer I had from their Chamber of Commerce to have executive-level Hispanics from the United States come visit for a free vacation of three whole days and see all the special places Puerto Rico had to offer for conventions. I was president of the Latino Association at work and because of this title was invited to see Puerto Rico on this level.

Those three days were filled with dancing under the stars, eating seafood on the beach with the warm breezes, and visiting four-star hotels. One hotel offered a bottle of Remi Martin, a sand castle with a palm tree made out of brown sugar and chocolate, and strawberries in our room. We saw professional dancers as entertainment, while the band members in their white tuxes with black ties played their music for floor shows. I even had the opportunity to see the Baseball Hall of Famer Juan Marichal as he signed for me four baseballs in one of the hotel lobbies. Other free gifts were high-quality terry cloth white bathrobes, original artwork of Puerto Rico-style houses, a painting, and a Puerto Rican cookbook. There was a theater production of *Actors: Ponce De Le Leon and the Pirates*. Stories were told to us by tour guides of how the women of San Juan, with their candles glowing in the night, followed the priests to let the invaders who were out on the shore think that they had many men who could fight them; their presence sent the invaders on their way. We ate lunch at the Governor's Palace, meeting lots of friendly and fun-loving people. To me, Puerto Rico was a fun-loving and generous country that rolled out the red carpet for us as tourists and visitors.

My soul sister Miranda is Puerto Rican, and I was able to share my memories of Puerto Rico with her. We talked about the town of Ponce, where her mother was born. I remember being in Ponce, where we visited a rum factory and saw a big hacienda and a beautiful open-garden patio with tropical plants.

Miranda is a member of our Kaiser Permanente Latino Association (KPLA). I met her while attending one of our award banquet dinners. We rapidly became friends due to her friendliness and openness to accept me in her social circle of friends. I discovered Miranda is very articulate, highly intelligent, and multitalented with leadership abilities; she performs outstanding work, whether it is for volunteerism or employment, and she is dependable. Miranda possesses a deep love for her daughter.

My husband, Jean-Pierre, and I were invited to come to Miranda's house for dinner on October 24, 2009, a Saturday, at 4:30 p.m. What we did not realize was that this dinner would transport us to Puerto Rico as we ate with Donnie and Miranda Sanz. The cuisine was Puerto Rican, and the dinner was most satisfying. When my mouth came in touch with the first tasting of the beans and rice, I knew the recipe was a traditional one. Miranda had told me it was her mother's bean recipe. I was literally transported to another place and time in Old San Juan. The beans were pinto, but unlike my style of cooking; they were delicate and one could tell it was authentic. As the taste of the beans reached my palate, I had an instant sensation of being in heaven. It was delicious, and I thought nothing could top the flavor of these beans.

The next wonderful treat was the serving of two different styles of plantains, one sweet and one served with a garlic and cilantro sauce. It had been many years since I had seen plantains being panfried on a stove. What I learned was that the green bananas called plantains were double-fried in olive oil and then served with a garlic sauce. The yellow bananas were the sweet ones, and they too were panfried. Both were out of this world to my taste buds. Red wine and green tossed salad were also served. But I could not get my mind off the pinto beans and their distinct flavor, and along with the plantains, my husband and I were in a little piece of heaven.

After dinner, I excused myself and visited their bathroom, only to see things that immediately reminded me of another time and place. First was a wooden box, placed on the sink countertop; it looked very similar to the type of wooden boxes my grandfather and my dad had at their homes. My grandfather used his wooden box for cigarettes and cigars, while my dad just collected them. The wooden boxes in Miranda's bathroom reminded me of my own family. The next item I noticed was a sun-shaped, wrought iron candleholder. I had received one very similar to this from a loyal employee whom I managed years ago; he died of AIDS. He was also Latino, and I was immediately reminded of him and wondered if he was visiting me at this moment.

When I entered the living room, I noticed two pairs of rosary beads and knew they were symbolic of someone who most likely had died; I did not want to pry by asking and changing the flavor of our coming together. I knew Miranda's mother had died recently and thought just maybe it was a spiritual collage about her, so I remained silent. I found out days later while talking to Miranda on the telephone that the rosary beads were from two funerals of a brother and sister who within two months had both died from domestic violence. Miranda had been given the rosary beads at their funerals. The beads were draped over a photo collage of her mother. This was important to me because I collect rosary beads, and it immediately reminded me of my fond affection for them when I saw them on display in Miranda's living room.

Miranda and I are both spiritually connected. One night I was at home glancing through the most recent issue of *Latina* magazine when a strong urge came over me to connect with Miranda, not the next day but at that very moment. I cannot explain it, but it was something I knew I had to do. As Miranda answered her phone, I told her about the strange feeling that overcame me to call her. She said that was very unusual because she was not in California but in New York City and that her mother was terminally ill. She had been just at the same time looking through her latest issue of *Latina* magazine as well. We were both amazed by this sudden coincidence, and I knew it was the right moment to connect with Miranda because she was in so much pain about her mother's terminal illness.

Just recently the same feeling came over me again to connect with Miranda. I left a phone message on her cell phone to tell her she was coming through loud and clear to me to connect with her and that I hoped she was all right. I felt she was struggling with making a life decision and that she needed someone to say whatever she decides, it will be the right choice. The next day Miranda called me and said this was exactly what she was going through and that my call helped her at this time of need.

I do not have an answer to any of this but only know to go with the flow when it happens. Because of the strong spiritual connection we share, I knew Miranda would be one of my selections as a soul sister. Miranda is much younger than I. However, unlike my other soul sisters who have given so much of themselves to me, I feel we are the gift to our younger soul sisters. We are here to encourage, inspire, and support them as they go through their own life experiences.

Here is Miranda's life story about a mother's love.

"A MOTHER'S LOVE"
by Miranda Sanz

"EN TODO QUE HACES VAS representando tu cultura y el carácter de tu raza, haga lo con pasion, Si viene del corazón siempre es recto."

"In all that you do, you are representing your culture and the character of your people, so do it with passion, and if it comes from the heart, it's always the right thing to do." —Millie Rodrigues

I was born at St. John's Hospital in Brooklyn, New York, on January 24, 1972. From what I understand, my mother went into labor; while she was laboring, there was a movie playing with a famous actress. She loved her so much she named me after her. She also named my brother after a famous singer. I don't know why, but for some reason my mother was starstruck. Interestingly enough, I aspired to be a star most of my life.

When I think about the character of my people and family ...

I'm trying to remember when I was back in Puerto Rico (PR) with my mother and my aunt. My mother did not meet her father until she was in her mid-thirties, and then she found out she had sixteen brothers and sisters that she didn't know. I was around seven years old, and it was my first trip to PR.

It was weird. The feeling I got throughout the island was a very loving and very passionate feeling. When Puerto Ricans party, it's like one big family, regardless of who you know. We are very festive and colorful people. Another example of that is we have *"fiesta patronales"* throughout the year, celebrating either a saint or just some significant event or hero for that specific town.

A fiesta patronal is a patriotic event, and it is amazing. There is food, music, dancing, and bands playing in the street. It goes on all weekend long, and in each town it takes place at different times of the year. I have been to a couple of them. My first fiesta patronal was really memorable because the artist that was singing was Celia Cruz. She was the queen of salsa. She grabbed my mother's hand and brought her up on stage with her to dance.

I would describe Puerto Ricans as welcoming, hospitable, colorful, sensitive, and very respectful. We have a tendency to always want to help people. *Pasión* for us is like a fire, a fire that burns without having to ignite it. It is almost like a desire to please, to fulfill something for someone, or to achieve something, but you cannot use that term for everything. We use it in so many different ways—with our partners to mean chemistry, with our friends to mean mutual love, and so on. When you use this term at work or at school, it means to do what you do with love to achieve the best possible outcome. When you do it passionately, you do it with your heart. It's your heart that is really leading you, and your brain is assisting. When you're doing something *con pasión*, it is the most fulfilling feeling.

I was raised Catholic and, of course, following Catholic traditions. My mother, I want to say, was a progressive Catholic. She was not a traditional Catholic; we weren't dragged to Mass every Sunday or forced to go to confession every Saturday, but we did do a lot of volunteering at the church. My mother always made sure we stayed connected. Actually most Saturdays, I was awakened by salsa music playing and my mother cooking breakfast, and then we would clean house all morning. Dancing and singing while cleaning makes chores so much more fun.

I did not finish my sacraments until after I had my daughter. Although we were not traditional Catholics, we had a strong sense of faith. Our value system is based on our faith, for example: girls do not do certain things, and only boys can do certain things. When I was growing up, I was the one who had to wash the dishes while my brothers went out to play. Girls were expected to learn how to cook and clean. I think things today have changed significantly. With the X'ers, the whole generational shift has encouraged Latinas to be who they want to be.

My father was very strict. I was not allowed to sit on the porch or go to my friend's house. If you were walking down the street with a gentleman, such as my father, the daughter or wife would never walk on the outside by the curb. They always had to be on the inside. My brothers got away with everything; I got away with nothing. If my father came home and the dishes were still in the sink, I would get in trouble. It was pretty tough, and there was a point in junior high school when I was not even allowed to look out of my bedroom window—I guess because my father was so fearful I would fall in love, which I did anyway, there was no way to stop that. I guess he was worried that boys were influencing me or maybe would knock me up. I am not really sure, but that was the way he was raised and in hindsight, he didn't know any different.

My paternal grandfather was what we call a *mujeriego*. a woman's man. I remember my grandfather not being with us for a while because he had left with another woman. He would live with her for a long time, and then he would come back to my grandmother. He was with us for a couple of years, and then he would go again. My grandmother always took him back; this was the way it was. The term *machismo*, it is like I said earlier: the woman had her place in the kitchen. It was expected for you to get married between ages eighteen to twenty. The idea was the man went out to work and the woman stayed home. My father's sister to this day does not know how to drive a car.

She ran away from her house to her husband's house. All she did was cook, clean, and raise her children.

In the Hispanic culture, the male role is the dominant role. You did what your husband said you should do, as men were the providers. Women were not allowed to work outside the home. The men were the ones who made the money, so they were the ones with the control. They were in control of what transpired in the home and with the children. It was a very demeaning role for women. The men show their love this way.

My father and I had a very strained relationship. I left my home at fifteen because I did not want to break up my mother's marriage. Through years of therapy, I found out this was the way he was raised. My grandfather was like this to his sister. There were generations of this particular family dynamic. So when I finally could accept it, I could empathize with my father. I began to realize my father did not know any other way to raise a son or a daughter. With the boys, it was really not that difficult: you took them fishing, and you threw them a ball on the baseball field. The key word was the "daughter." I guess thinking about his daughter and her leaving home was hard for him to accept.

My mother, on the other hand, never thought of herself as a traditional Puerto Rican woman. She went to school and worked most of my adolescent life, yet she was always there for every event, every milestone. She learned how to drive because she didn't want to depend on my father to take her or us everywhere. I guess that's where I get my energy from. I admired my mother and never wanted to disappoint her. She was the only one in the world who understood who I really am and never judged me for it. I could tell her anything, and she would just say, "Mita, I love you no matter what." (Mita is her nickname for me.) It's that unconditional love that kept me truthful. I never wanted her to hear something about me or something I was doing from someone else. I would rather face the consequences that came with whatever it was than to look at her face if she heard it from a third party.

I am raising my daughter with the same principles. She can tell me anything—no judgments and don't ever lie because I will be so disappointed if I find out the truth later. If my daughter comes to tell me something she did or something that happened, I just listen and then ask questions to gauge what she thinks is right or wrong. Like my mom did with me. That was/is my mother's love.

I think in order to be culturally sensitive, even among Hispanics there are differences in the words we use throughout Latin America. Words that are jokingly used in one Latin country can be offensive in another. For example, Mexicans frequently use the word *cabron*, and to us that means something that is very, very bad. They use it as a term of endearment, a slang word that is thrown around a lot. To Puerto Ricans, it means that your spouse is cheating on you and you know it—you have no respect for yourself.

To me, what is offensive is to assume I'm one thing or the other. For example, to assume that I'm a Mexican, Cuban, Colombian, or Puerto Rican, or to assume that I belong to some category because I have olive skin, dark eyes, and dark hair is not correct. It isn't fair to categorize me or to stereotype me. I think all the Latino countries have good and bad, and they all are beautiful but in different ways. For someone to assume that I eat *frijoles* every day for breakfast just does not sit well with me. Puerto Ricans do not eat tortillas. We don't think it's a bad thing; it's just not part of our cuisine. So when you look at me, don't assume I eat tortillas with every meal. We do not eat refried beans. We do not call beans *frijoles*; we call them *habichuelas*.

In regard to the Spanish language, there are lots of different dialects and lots of different rhythms to them. Puerto Ricans are known for talking very fast. In the Mexican culture, people tend to draw their Spanish out. This makes it a little different or harder for me to understand sometimes. Peruvians do not speak fast or slow; it is almost melodic. How can I describe it? I have a lot of Peruvian friends right now. I am engrossed in this culture, and it is amazing to me. I have a friend who is my mechanic. He has become a citizen, he owns a business and his home, and he has become very successful. Their melodic tone is interesting to me. Then there are Dominicans who speak like Italians, with lots of expression. The rate of speed and the way they say their R's like Brazilians who speak Portuguese, like the sound "TH" sounds very different. I want to say it is "spicy." It is like the Spanish language is all over the place.

What I have learned to do is to just ask, "So, what does this mean to you?"

What does it mean to be Hispanic? My answer is that we are a very proud culture in general and across borders. We try very hard to be good citizens; and for me, to be a good citizen is to be a representative of your culture and your people.

Other people tend to see us as coming off very forward. We are not forward; we just feel a need to speak for the underdog, whether it be Hispanic, African American, or Asian. Again, we have a tendency to want to help. I see that in all my Latino friends. I see that when I go to Puerto Rico, which I consider my country. We want to save the world too.

There is a country song that expresses what I hope for. It is not written by Leeann Womack, but she sings it and it is called, "I Hope You Dance." The words in that song contain a message every mother I think would want to tell their child. I found it when my mother passed; I'm going to cry now. After I came back from the funeral, I went to Kmart looking for a book for my daughter. There was actually a book written about this song, and there was a CD of the song in the back of the book. The line in the song that I would want my daughter to know is, "Do not fear the mountains in the distance, and never let a broken heart leave you bitter." I think those are the two things I want her to know. I hope you dance and don't sit it out.

When my maternal grandmother, whom I did not care for, passed, I went back to Puerto Rico to help my mother with the funeral. I told her, "I'm not going to stay with you because I am going to stay in Old San Juan; I want to see my country. I want to learn about my history and my ancestry." I met my great-aunt on my mother's side of the family. Her name is Lucy, and she is an amazing woman. She traced our ancestry back to Italy. Apparently our great-great-great-grandfather came from Italy, and for some reason they stopped in Puerto Rico. That is how my grandmother's family on my mother's side got started.

I do not know a whole lot about my father's side of the family. He was born in Puerto Rico in a small fisherman's town, and my mother was born in a small town they call *pueblo de las quenepa*. *Quenepa* is a fruit that comes off a tree; it is very tasty though bitter, with a furry texture. The food is the thing I love most about Puerto Rico. My mom took me there almost every summer as a child, and my fondest memories involve food.

My mother was the extended family matriarch, especially with my cousins. There was a point when my mother was the savior aunt to all my cousins. When you were in trouble, you went to Titi Millie's (*titi* means aunt) so she could get you out of the pickle you got yourself into. I remember there was a time when my cousin (who will remain anonymous) called my mom from jail. Actually, even my mother's younger brothers did that as well every time they got pinched. My cousin had gotten caught with a gun. My mom, of course, took care of it for him. The gun wasn't his and wasn't even in his possession. The police officer found it in a bush my cousin ran past, but only after the kid whom it belonged to ran past the bush and threw it there. Lucky my mom worked for the New York Police Department and understood the system.

I am a very spiritual person, and I can always feel my mother and sometimes my maternal grandfather. He visits me, and I know it because I can smell him around me. It is usually when I'm in bed at night when I'm worried or obsessing about something. For some reason, a calm will come to me, and I know what to do—if I should just let it go, or if I need to take a specific action. I can feel it in my chest. I smell my mother a lot. My daughter also smells my mother. This is really funny, but everybody to me has their own scent. My mother has her own scent. I can smell her a mile away; it is not perfume but her own scent. I could always smell her, and that's how I know she is with me. I'll get a feeling and I cannot sleep, which means I have to get up and take action on something. As for my grandfather, I can almost hear his rocking chair; when I met him the first time, he was sitting in the rocking chair. I could hear the "creak" of his rocking chair. It feels like a comfort, but what gets frustrating is when I need them to come to me and they don't. I know my mother is probably saying to me right now, "Mita, you just have to get over it!"

In my younger years, we were always at my grandmother's house in Harlem. It seems like every holiday we were there. It was super Hispanic, which is why it's called "Spanish" Harlem. It seems like we were always there at Christmas and Thanksgiving, every major holiday. The house was always filled with some kind of salsa or merengue music playing either on the hi-fi or the radio. I remember being in my grandmother's kitchen and grating coconuts to make *cocito*, which is the Puerto Rican version of eggnog. The base is coconut milk, rum, cinnamon, and vanilla—all the good stuff that is really bad for you. I remember grating *platanos* for *pastelles*, our version of tamales. We make it during the holidays by grating the bananas and the potatoes, sitting with these big bowls between our legs. The family would sit us down with these big bowls between our legs with the *guayo*. We would sit there and grate for hours. So like Mexicans mashing corn for mesa, we were grating bananas and potatoes. There was this wonderful smell of *aroz con dulce* coming out of the oven. It is our version of a rice pudding, full of cinnamon, raisins, and, oh, my God, it is so sweet we call it "rice candy." My mother would always save the husk of the coconut so we could eat the meat after we squeezed it all out and grated it. My childhood was always filled with family coming together, parties, and baseball parks. My brothers always played baseball, and my mom coached.

To me, there is a huge difference living in New York because it is like a race; everyone is in a hurry to go nowhere. It's a difference for me personally; I do not feel a sense of community there. Everyone there lives in their own silos. It is just such a fast pace. I grew up there and I love New York City, but I have never felt like I belong there.

Being Hispanic here in the Bay Area, I think we aspire to be more. This might be just what I have seen. They do not aspire to be more specifically in my neighborhood. Here the Latinas aspire to be something. I think of my Latino friends, and I cannot think of anyone in my old neighborhood that I would want to be like; we did not have role models. It's so different here; it is way more relaxed. Believe it or not, we are really relaxed here.

The only thing that was surprising to me was when I felt discriminated against. I had never felt or experienced racism. I was followed in a store by a manager or someone who was hired by the store, and it made me feel like a criminal. I have been ignored when waiting to be served, and then someone white comes in and they serve them, leaving me waiting. It was really kind of alarming to me because I had never felt that in my life. Living in New York or in Los Angeles, I had never felt that; but living in the San Francisco area, I feel it here.

My mother was my life. When growing up, I did not see much of my father because he worked a lot. So there are a lot of gaps in my memory. I probably remember my father more when I was growing up in middle school and as a teenager, as opposed to when I was younger. He wasn't around very much. My mother did everything, though. She was the PTA president for I do not know how long at our school. She coached my brother's baseball teams. She actually sold Tupperware in my young years until I went to middle school. She was good at it; she got a station wagon, and she was sent to Florida. My mother was a good saleswoman with her charisma.

My father did not come to graduations or school functions. My brother graduated from the same school my father graduated from, and he did not go to his graduation. I think that was in part the way he was raised by his father. My mother always chalked it up that he worked nights and that he was tired, but after a while you just did not question it or expect it. That was the way we kind of lived with our father; we just did not expect much.

The people who were most significant to me are my mother and my mother's younger brother Harold. He died very young, God rest his soul; he taught me about music, how to dance and sing. They said he died of cancer; he was in his mid-forties when he died. My mother was young, too, when she passed. Other major influences were my cousin Lisa; she's like an older sister. She's my cousin on my father's side of the family. My godmother (*mi madrina*) was always a huge influence. She was not always present, but her advice and counsel were there when needed. To this day, I cannot leave New York without stopping by to see her. She was present at family functions, but she was not in my everyday life. Every time I needed something for some reason, she was always there. There was never a time when my mother didn't tell me, "Your madrina asked for you." She'd say, "You should call your madrina" or "Your madrina left you something." She always stayed connected. My godfather has not been around for quite some time, but she was always there. I always knew I would have my madrina.

I think I'm good and bad when it comes to raising my daughter the way I was raised. My ex-husband was always absent because he was always working until he was laid off. He would leave sometimes at five in the morning and not be home until dinnertime or after.

Traditions started with Christmas at my mother's house. Christmas is a big deal with my mother and me. My mother went to school and worked pretty much most of my adolescent life, and I have inherited that characteristic.

Every year the day after Thanksgiving, the house was decorated. Mother worked the swing shift, from 3:00 to 11:00 p.m., and every year she would come home from work and the whole house would be lit up. That tradition continued even after I left New York; she kept doing it.

My mother worked for the New York City Police Department as a police attendant in central booking. She processed the prisoners' paperwork and monitored the females while they housed them until the arraignment. She hurt her arm, back, and neck when a female prisoner resisted being put in a cell.

I'm currently a senior consultant with a healthcare organization. I have a bachelor of science degree in business administration and a master's degree in business administration. I enjoy singing and dancing; I salsa dance almost every weekend. I was singing with a band in San Francisco on Monday and Wednesday nights. I was just with my bandleader last night, and I met a guy who has a band. He took my phone number, and he may want me for his band. It is salsa music. But before that, when I first came to California, I used to sing at the Oakland Hilton on Saturday nights for about a year and a half. I also enjoy the creativeness of the craft of painting statuary. I write poetry now and then. I'm multitalented. I enjoy computer applications, but mostly I love being with my daughter.

The difference I would like to make in the world is to influence or mentor one person, such as a young Latina, so that there would be one more role model for my daughter. I want to touch them and let them know they can do it. To encourage them to stop listening to others who say, "No, you can't." That was what happened to me; my father said I couldn't. My middle brother said I couldn't. It was either I was not good enough or it was just not going to happen. Lo and behold, I was the only one of his children that graduated with a college degree. My father did make an exception and came to my graduations. He did not go to my brother's graduation, but he came to both of mine.

What I want others to know about my people and me is, "Don't discredit us; don't sell us short." You would be amazed at what we can do and what we can accomplish. You have to be better than the best, or you are not taken seriously. If you show a little more boldness or assertiveness, you are considered as "brash."

There are two types of Latinas. This is going to sound weird, but I grew up with astrology playing a very big role in my life. I was raised Catholic, but my mother believed in what we call *santeria*. It is a very spiritual practice, and so I think a lot of astrology plays into it. When I think about the two different types of Latinas—the silent one and the bold one, or the subservient one to the more vocal one—I think it has to do with how you were raised. My cousin Lisa turned out the way she did because my mother was in her life. Her mother was very subservient. Lisa now lives in Florida and has four children. She is a postal worker and delivers the mail. She is married to a wonderful man, but she is independent. She drives a car, she takes care of her family, and she contributes to the household. I really strongly feel that if my mother had not been in my cousin's life, she could have turned out like my aunt, her mother. So that is the difference: it is the women you have in your life that make a difference in how you grow up. This probably applies to any culture. So don't discredit yourself; do not sell yourself short, which we do a lot. We are our own worst enemy.

I want to do my best because I'm an overachiever. This is part of passion, and people don't get it. The only ones who do get it think like me. I think something that offends me is people who discredit it or dismiss it. A lot of times, I have found out that they say, "Shoot, I made a mistake because I discredited that; I probably should have paid more attention to that." Like I said, my mother was the biggest influence on me in everything she did. She wanted it to be her best, and she wanted your best.

My mother died of liver failure after a liver transplant fourteen years ago. I think Mother was tired, tired of people telling her what to do, tired of medication and blood draws every month. She got tired of people telling her not to drink soda because of the diabetes she contracted from the prednisone. I think that is why she stayed in Puerto Rico for a year by herself after her mother died. She was done with people.

When we were in Puerto Rico for my mother's funeral, people were saying things about her. It's interesting that when people die, all others tend to do is gossip. They were talking about how my mother was drinking beer in her condition. There are bigger sins in life than my mother drinking beer. At that point in my mother's life, she really did not care anymore. She got tired of people telling her what to do. My father had a really hard time with that. I remember we were in the car together, and he said, "I'm so angry that she did that. Why did she have to do that?" I looked at him and said, "It is not about you. She was tired after twelve years of this." All the ups and downs, and I think it was because my brothers and father did not manage her care.

When she landed in the hospital, one of the things my family said was they never thought this would happen again. I managed her care. I took care of her the whole time from the beginning to the end. When my mother got sick, I was about twenty-two years old. I was living in New York and going to school until right before I turned twenty-four. I cared for my mother. This was the time after the transplant. She got sick really suddenly, and we thought it was the stomach flu. One day I came home from school, and I noticed she was yellow. I said, "Mommy, something is wrong." We took her to the general practitioner, and he admitted her *immediately* to the hospital. They could not figure out what was wrong with her, so they transferred her to Brookdale Hospital. She was there for another week, and then she went into a hepatic coma. By the time they figured out what was wrong, they transferred her to Mount Sinai. She only had forty-eight hours to live, so she went right to the top of the transplant list. Luckily she got a transplant, and then she had twelve more years with us.

I want to be known for "There's one of the good ones … a loving, caring, and compassionate person. She was someone who gave back to the community and someone who impacted someone's life. She did something to touch someone's life."

"Never limit yourself because of others' limited imagination; never limit others because of your own limited imagination."
—Mae Jemison, astronaut

Jone Johnson Lewis, "About.com Women's History."
Accessed December 22, 2010.
http://womenshistory.about.com/od/quotes/a/mae_jemison.htm>.

INTRODUCING SOUL SISTER
STEPHANIE RIVERA

STEPHANIE IS MY MOST RECENT soul sister. I first met Stephanie at a Kaiser Permanente Latino Association (KPLA) chapter meeting in Walnut Creek. She was one of the speakers presenting a leadership development program for others who were present in the room. Her presentation was well prepared, and as she began to speak, I realized that there was something about her I wanted to know more about. It was the strangest feeling that was coming over me, and I sat in my chair and listened carefully. After the meeting, I knew I wanted to go up to her and introduce myself. As I approached her and our hands met for the first time while I looked into her eyes, it was as if I was getting in touch with her soul. There was a deep feeling that kept pounding in my head saying I had to know her better. It was as if I was getting a spiritual message from above; to pick up on my intuitiveness and follow up with this person, I needed to know more about her. It is a very difficult feeling to place into words, but it was truly something I did not feel with anyone else whom I met in my business or personal world. It was if a special message was coming over me, and I needed to follow up with it.

Months later, when I decided to write a book about soul sisters, I thought about inviting Miranda as a soul sister to come to my house and see if she was interested in joining us. For some strange reason, I thought to ask Miranda about having an "alternate" Latina to be a replacement if for some reason Miranda were unable to participate at every meeting. Interestingly enough, I did not have this feeling or thought about any of the other soul sisters besides Miranda.

My first thought was to appoint Stephanie as an alternate. Miranda agreed this was a very good choice for us, and for some reason in my head and heart, I knew Stephanie would accept the invitation to be a coauthor of *Soul Sisters, Come on to My House.*

In addition to knowing Stephanie and the wonders of this very special woman, I had the great opportunity to experience a quinceanera not once but twice through Stephanie's daughters' invitations. Each event was special and educational for me since I had never experienced going to a quinceanera before. It is truly a grand affair, like a wedding but with the innocence of a young lady becoming a woman. Each of Stephanie's three daughters was dressed beautifully in white dresses and had young men in tuxes as their escorts. Another special part of the ceremony and preparation is that many family and friends partake in the planning and ceremony. They purchase gifts for the special event, such as dresses, shoes, jewelry, cake, candles, and flowers. This makes it special because it is inclusive of the family and friends of the hostess and her daughters. After the religious ceremony, there are dancing, singing, and entertainment. We all are seated to a wonderful dinner, and the celebration goes on into the night.

Little did I know at the time of meeting Stephanie Rivera that my understanding of migrant and seasonal workers in the fields would never be the same again. Through knowing and growing to love Stephanie for the wonderful, courageous woman she is, I learned the real story of the grape. California wine is revered as world-class, and yet there are invisible men, women, and children who struggle to survive in those fields. I'm sure you will agree with me how special and unique this woman is. Again, I hope to provide a resting place for Stephanie when she needs emotional support and the comfort of compassionate listening. I selected Stephanie as a soul sister for her ability to continue with life even when all is crashing around her. She has great courage and ability to achieve her greatest dreams. Stephanie is already a great success within herself, having overcome numerous obstacles.

Here is the incredible story of Stephanie Rivera.

"IF YOU WANT TO LIVE, YOU HAVE TO EARN IT!"
by Stephanie Rivera

I WAS BORN IN DINUBA, California, a small rural town that had about six thousand people. Now I think there are eight thousand people living there. My mom is the third oldest child of nine kids, and I'm the oldest of three. My mom had me as an unwed mother, and during this time it was not acceptable to have a child out of wedlock. So when I was born, we lived with my grandparents. It was a large extended family that I lived with.

My family was migrant farmworkers before I was born. A few years before I was born, my grandfather bought a small plot of land and built a house on it. Before that, my family had lived in a very small house. It was at this time when they became migrant workers. Migrant farmworkers follow the crops of the season. So if it's time to pick lemons, they go to the Central Valley and pick lemons. Then if it is time to pick apples, they go to Washington and pick apples. When it is time to pick potatoes, they go to Idaho to pick potatoes there. Then when it is August and time to pick grapes (a big thing, since there are both Napa and table grapes), the families will come here to work. These migrant farmworkers follow the crops. My mom did that, but when I was born, her family became "seasonal" workers; that means they stay where they are, and they are able to stay in one place to harvest all the different crops because they are surrounded by such a variety of crops.

My mother was born in Selma, California, in 1947. She was a young mother, about twenty or twenty-one when I was born. She worked in the fields as a child, and because her family was migrant farmworkers, her schooling was very fractured. My mother's family was traveling all the time. They traveled up through Gilroy, California, a lot to pick cotton awhile, and then they had to go up through Washington State. I was not born during this time, and I do not have this experience. As a child she was born into it because her parents, my grandparents, were migrant workers also. My grandfather was part Puerto Rican, and his mother was a drinker. I did not hear much about her; I don't know much about that generation because that kind of information is always a secret. My maternal great-grandmother, I did know her because she lived with us for a while. I lived with my grandparents, and then my mom moved out, but all my aunts and uncles lived within a one- or two-mile radius of us. You have to remember these were small towns so my great-grandmother was around my grandmother the most, and I remember her. I remember when she fell, hurt her hip, and could not get to the front door. I was knocking on the door. I had to go tell my mom she would not come to the door. I was probably about eleven years old at the time. My great-grandmother was a very small woman, tiny and round. I think she was an orphan, so I did not know about her parents. However, my grandmother was born in Death Valley, California.

Everyone always makes the assumption about Latinas that your family is from Mexico. I'm actually a fourth-generation Californian, and I worked in the fields. My great-grandmother, grandmother, mother, and I all worked in the fields.

Not all Latinos are from Mexico; this assumption is a misconception. We still have family in Mexico, but most of my family is here in California. My grandmother's mom was the only girl in her family. I did not know that until she was passing away and I met my Tio Lupe from Mexico. He was a wonderful gentleman, and there were six in their family. There are third and fourth cousins who live in River Bank, California, and Modesto, California. Since I was around my grandparents so much I got to know a lot of the extended family. In all honesty, there is no distinction between family and extended family. I have hundreds of family members in the Central Valley of California.

One thing I have come to realize is the way I was born and how hard it must have been on my mom. I was born to a single mom at a time when it was not okay in a small town, and that was very hard for her. I can now see how hard that was for her to have to tell her parents that she was pregnant and my dad had left her. Additionally, to have my dad deny me and my existence has been hurtful to me, but it must have been devastating to my mom. At the time I was growing up, I could not imagine what it was like for her and the names that she was called and the sacrifices she made for me. I think I owe her a phone call.

The women in my life are very special to me. My grandmother loved me unconditionally and never complained about anything. My grandmother would get up and make the tortillas, the potatoes, and the meat to make sure everyone had their lunch. I never realized how much work that was. Today we just put a box of cereal on the table. Oh my goodness, I never realized the work that was involved in what these women did. They made sure there was food on the table and that we had clothes to wear. I'm not trying to romanticize it because there was another thing that happens with poverty: there is alcoholism and all sorts of other things happening, such as domestic violence. My mother sacrificed her life to be a mom to me and my siblings. My *tias* (aunts) loved me as well.

The men in my life are also dear to me. My grandfather took me in as his own daughter and helped raise me. My uncles also loved me. All in all I was surrounded by people who loved me. One lesson that I learned is that while I was loved, poverty meant that hard work was a necessity and regardless of age, this was my reality.

As a kid, the next thing I knew was I was thrown into this world and learned that if you want to live, you have to earn it. I was about six years old and had just started school. The interesting thing about harvesting grapes is that it seared into my brain. Maybe it was because of the hot sun at 115 degrees. Imagine: you are in this long row, and it is like when you are in the movies, and you are running down this long hallway and the hallway never ends. That's what it feels like because it is just always there. It is so hot, and it is as long as the eyes can see. You are only a kid, and you think, "What did I do?" There is dirt, and there are bees—I certainly remember the bees.

This was in the 1970s, so there was starting to be some awareness of pesticides but it was not like it is now. I liked the morning because it was cool and you could get a lot done. I was young, and I would say okay and would share a row of grapes. This was my summer vacation, and that is what I would do on vacation—go and pick grapes. I picked grapes sometimes for the whole day. What you really wanted to do was get out by three o'clock because that is the peak of the heat. But your job was to finish that row, so you had to stay until you finished that row, no matter what. It did not matter how hard or hot it was. So if you were good at picking grapes, then, of course, you were assigned your own row. As a kid, you did not think about it; you just did it.

I had my own row at the age of eight. I was in the fields until I was about fourteen, and then I went into the packinghouse. It's a big deal to get into the packinghouse because you are not out in the dirt. You are packing the fruit, but you are not in the dirt; your status is raised. There is shelter over your head, and there is an air-conditioner. Some of the larger packinghouses had air-conditioners, it was clean inside, and you had a break room.

My thought while I was working was, *How do you survive this, and not just survive?* I was about age eight or ten when my thinking began to shift. Mentally I thought there was a refuge and my refuge was school. Because school was easy, it was fun, it was indoors, it was clean, and to me that was what you did. Schooling was easy, like taking tests and writing. It was a snap; it was just like nothing.

I always picked grapes during summer breaks. I think we only did picking on weekends a few times. I actually felt fortunate because there were kids who had to pick grapes before school and did not have time to take a shower before they came to school; that is just not okay.

It is interesting that you are in an environment where everyone is in that environment but in very different ways. You had people who were undocumented, others who were born here but still doing that work who were migrants so you never really saw them and they were invisible, and then you had people who are born here who were seasonal. It is interesting that as I'm writing, this is how the mind shift probably came to me. I thought to myself, *I will not be invisible; you are not going to forget who I am.* At age eight, I thought that to myself, and that was part of me changing my own destiny. I was destined to be something, but what was that going to be? And I said to myself, "I'll be damned if this is where I'll end up." I would never put people down, but I also knew there was more to life than this.

Part of my mental shift came when I recognized the hierarchy of the world. There were the farmers who owned the land, and their families, the undocumented families, and the families who were USA born and we all went to school together. When I made the decision to not be invisible, I made another decision: you were going to respect me. Even to this day, when I get my professional evaluations at work, my leader says for some reason this respect thing sticks with you. I will just nod my head and say, "One day I'll tell you the story." I went to school with people who owned the land, and I would say to myself, *How in the hell did they do it? How do you get enough money to own your own land and to have all this too?* So I went to school with all of them who were in some way connected to the business of working the land.

My survival story is how I was going to survive the next moment. In many ways, it is like peeling an onion one layer at a time. One part is living in a single-parent home, the next part is the education, the next part is living in poverty, and then the final part is the spiritual. We were not Catholic by religion. I have two or three *tias* who are Catholic. Then I have people in my family that are Pentecostal, and we were baptized Methodists, so we acknowledged all of that. Then there was alcoholism, and I would say, "How do I survive this?" and "How do I survive the hush-hush stuff and all the family secrets?"

So I think for me, I got to a point to try and survive everything. I was focused on school, I was focused on work, and I had to take care of the people who lived with me and the parenting of myself too. My mother, who had such a difficult life, was not very nurturing so I began to work, work, work. I worked at the packinghouse at night, and during the day, I would babysit for my uncle and aunt. Another summer, I lived with my Tia Esther, and I would work with her daughter, my cousin, in the packinghouse. I was just working and going to school, working and going to school, and that is just what I did. This was my life.

I wanted to stay in school, but I did not know what that meant. I just kept working, going to school and praying. During this time, I recognized that the spiritual side was important as well for me because I wanted to go to church. Then at some point, my mom's faith was tested and I could see that she started to lose her faith in God. I had a sister and a younger brother who watched this as well. My younger brother's father was a substance abuser, and my mother got a lot of judgmental comments for her decisions. I was not the easiest child, and I was probably very judgmental of her. I regret that now. She at some point probably would say, "There is no God. If there was a God, he would not be doing this to me!"

All of a sudden, she did not go to church anymore. I think internally she just gave up. I did not know how to deal with it, so I just kept going to church. Then I went to another church, and it had a huge youth group membership. I remember this church because it was robust; it was a Mennonite church. I was in junior high school at the time, and I was very involved in this youth group. At Christmas they would give us a Christmas tree. I would go on trips with the youth group, and I was able to go to the Grand Canyon. It was the only way I was able to see different things.

I started to "grow wings." I say this because I started to connect with my teachers. Even my very first teacher came to my high school graduation; she gave me a picture of myself, a coffee cup, and a Bible. I still have the mug to this day. It says, "Your whole day is a rainbow," and I still have the Bible she gave to me. Then there were my first grade, second grade, third grade, fourth grade, fifth grade, and sixth grade teachers, all of whom were special to me. This special relationship with my teachers continued through junior high school and high school. One teacher, the biology teacher, saw something in me; his wife was the math teacher, but math was not my strength. I was never the valedictorian in class, but I was always just below them. The biology teacher would ask me, "What are you going to do when you graduate?" I said to him, "I guess I will go to Fresno State." He then asked, "Why are you going to do that?"

My mother actually had gone a little to college but never finished. She said, "Do you really want to go to Fresno State? It might be a little too close for you because you need your freedom." My mother pushed me all the time, and with her I never felt like I was good enough. Since there were teachers asking me, "What are you going to do?" I applied all over to different colleges. "If you want to stay in the area," one teacher said, "you could stay with my mother and go to the community college, which is nearby. When you come back home, you can take care of my mom." So he offered me alternatives. He had an elderly mother who lived next to a community college. I could go to school for two years and receive free room and board for taking care of his mom.

I just did not know what to do. I thought about getting a certified nursing certificate and my teacher offered to legally pay me. The funny thing about all of this was that I never thought about how I was going to pay for all of this.

My mother had since got a job as an eligibility worker, and I was under the illusion that colleges would somehow not have any funding for me. I had no idea about scholarships, grants, or student loans.

I realized how different I was when I recognized that there are people who take a vacation, they actually do go somewhere. We did not do that; our vacations and summers were the fields and the packinghouses. I started to think this was not okay. It just got to the point where there had to be something better. For me, I just knew I had to keep going to school even though I did not know where it was going to take me. I had no idea where "Oz" was, but school was my "yellow brick road." How I was going to pay for it, who knew and who cared?

Finally one recruiter came from the Santa Cruz area, and she gave me an application for financial aid. I said, "But my mom makes too much money." She said to me, "I do not think so." She told me to fill the application out and highlighted what I needed to fill out. So I applied at Santa Cruz because she was there. I ended up getting into Santa Cruz, and then I ended up getting into Fresno State.

I also got into UC Davis, and my biology teacher said, "If you are going to go to a UC, you should go to UC Davis." I asked, "Why?" He said, "You will adapt much better. There is danger in you going to some place that is so different, and at UC Davis, you will understand that work because the school is built on agriculture. It is a small place. You can ride your bike, and you will fall into place there." I did not have a clue where UC Davis was, and I did not know the significance of going to a UC campus. My grades were good enough to be just dropped off there without going first to a summer program to get adjusted.

When I was first dropped off at the UC Davis campus, I realized how different my own life had been. My first year at UC Davis was one of the hardest years of my life. I never felt like such an outcast. I never felt so alone. I never felt like a farmworker until I was out of that environment. I was in a dorm where people had gone to summer programs together so they all knew each other. I did not know anybody.

It was one of the loneliest experiences in my life. It was really hard, so I thought back to my earlier life. I was just like that kid again. How do I survive this? What do I do now? And always there was another test for me. I have to say, most people in my family didn't understand the college process. My mother did not understand what I was going through, plus my grandmother was ill. People in my family did not understand, and hell, I did not understand what I was trying to do. There were times I just said, "Screw it. Maybe I should just go home, become something I was destined to be. I'm stupid." I was starting to question who I was. I said to myself, *How dare I question, try* and be something, or even think I could be something different? What makes me think I could come out of the fields and really be successful? How stupid am I? I was also questioning what success really means. I never wanted to put myself back into a situation where I did not fit again. I was not one of the smartest kids, and I was not one of the dumbest kids. I was eighteen when I began school at UC Davis.

My financial aid did not come in, and the cafeteria lady took mercy on me and fed me. My grandfather bought me a bike for transportation. I do not know how I got through that first year of school. Then I started to meet some people, and I really liked them a lot. They were incredible, and they were fun. I then started to say I needed to regroup and figure this out, and so I did. I even found a job that paid me.

I received a bachelor's of science degree from UC Davis in 1990. I received a master's in public health in 1992 from UC Berkeley. I was ready for Berkeley when I got there. I was twenty-one when I started that program. I had a master's degree by the age of twenty-three. I was the only one in my family at the time to graduate with a college degree.

Some traditions are good and some are bad in my family. Everything in my family centers on food. The first rain of the season, my grandmother would make albondigas soup (meatball soup) and homemade tortillas. When I'm sick, that is what I crave.

The biggest thing for me is that there is a *God*. That may sound simple, but for me that was big. I would question God just like that book, *"Are you there, God? It's me, Margaret."* I would say to God, "You're ignoring me, and I'm invisible to you." Even now as an adult, I think that way sometimes. But I changed it a little bit, so now I say, "I know you are there. I know you're listening. I do not know what path you have chosen for me. I have no idea what I'm supposed to do."

If I could do anything I wanted, I would sit and have a cup of coffee with God. I would ask him, "What do you want from me? What were you trying to tell me that I could not hear? Or that I did not listen to. What was it? Tell me as a father, what is it?" That is very important because at this point, I realize there is a God. I have always felt that way even when I questioned, "Is there a God?" Then I changed my thoughts to, "There is a God, but are you listening to me? God, have you forgotten me?"

To me, "soul" means having heart in what you do. The world to me is very superficial. People will tell you whatever they think you want to hear in order to get whatever they want from you. But when people go out of their way to give you a call, send you a text, or give you a gift, that is having heart and soul. Like anything you do, it is done with heart. It means a lot, and that is what "soul" means, despite culture, class, or race. Remember, I had to grow up

146

ignoring all that. A soul sister means to me somebody who may not have the same experience but has the same feelings. It is someone without judgment.

When I think about what is "just," that is really hard to answer. I really believe the statement that life is not fair. Bad things happen to good people. What is just is when you are able to still stand afterward and still be surrounded by the people who are there and know that you are loved.

My family means everything to me. My family means a lot, not just my children, but the people who have my heart—that's what family means to me. Family means people whom I love dearly. The biggest thing is that love should be unconditional. There should not be any strings attached to it, and that comes with forgiveness and patience. I have not been good at any of this because I always felt like I had to "earn" love and be a good student, daughter, sister, cousin, etc. I was loved if I was an A student, but what if I was shoveling horse manure, would you still love me? I'm hoping that the people around me would still love me. I just want people to know that when you put conditions on love, that is not love.

Cultural sensitivity is not everyone believing in the same thing. Respecting someone is not like, "I like you, and we are all of the same mind-set." To me, when you stop treating people like they are people and stop respecting them as human beings, that is probably the worst thing you can do to another human being. When you see and hear people talk about undocumented workers going back to where they came from because this is "our America," it is wrong. It is not just because it is insensitive or disrespectful. You are to respect another human being with dignity because they are alive, they have a heart, and they are doing their best. It is not your issue to deal with it. Cultural sensitivity people take it to say it is about culture, about class; what it's really about is treating a person like a human being.

My experience with interracial marriage comes from my own background of just having to survive and connect. I have never pigeonholed people. I think if you give people space, it will surprise you how much you can learn. When I was single, the person I thought I was going to marry was from a different race. It was really important to me to love yourself, and that comes from your parents or your siblings, someone who can impact your life. But ultimately you have to love yourself, and a lot of people don't. A lot of us struggle with that, and we think we will be loved if we are what society expects of us to be. An interracial marriage just challenges that to another level. You're saying, "I do not care what anybody thinks. I'm going to follow the path that works for me." The part that people need to be careful about is sometimes you can do that as a rebellious thing, which is not the thing to do. But if you are really and truly in love with someone else who is of a different race, you simply say, "This is the path I choose to take." You need to know that sometimes it can be a lonely path; sometimes people do not embrace that, so you have to learn how to embrace yourself—the good, the bad, and the ugly.

I was married to a man for many, many years, and I took my vows very seriously. He and I were very different but we learned from each other. I felt like I was still "surviving" in this marriage, as we endured so much in so little time. He was very ill and almost died until he received his heart transplant. We had ten more years together, and I am very blessed for all of my children. I have two older stepdaughters, and four children of my own. I learned early on that children are a blessing, but that God just lent them to me for a while. They are on their own path and have to find their way in the world, and all I can do is love them unconditionally. When you have children, they have to feel good about themselves. They have their story too.

I never wanted my children to think they are parenting themselves or that they are not loved unconditionally. It was very important to me; and after the death of my husband, I think they know that. They have taken on a lot of responsibility, especially my two older daughters, who are twins. All of them have taken on so much, and it breaks my heart. In addition, they are the product of an interracial marriage. I have four children and two older children who were my husband's daughters but they lived with us. In my heart, they are my children. There was a lot around that, and they were also a product of an interracial marriage. The kids could all tell you what it is like being an interracial child, but that is a whole other book. That is probably some of the most interesting dynamics, for them to tell their stories.

Their stories are really about how good they feel about being a person. They are challenged on that every day. They get daily comments like, "We do not believe your mother is Mexican. How can you have a quinceanera?" They are put to the test every day that they walk into a classroom and every day that they walk into a job. My daughters put down they are Hispanic and African American. When my son cut his hair, people said to him, "Oh, now you look like a little Hispanic boy." He said, "I have always been a Hispanic boy."

So they have to feel good about themselves as people—that is what I try to instill in my kids. When you feel good about yourself, you can tolerate it; when you do not feel good about yourself, that is when you are judgmental, critical, and not compassionate. So in life, my circle around me reflects that, and it is because this is whom I love dearly. My view on the world when you ask about interracial marriage is that it is the children who can tell you about it best. The two people who are married to each other still have their own identities. My husband was very sensitive to the Hispanic culture. He learned how to cook Hispanic food. I celebrate the quinceaneras because it was a big thing to my children. My husband liked the tradition about it because of the fact it was acknowledging their background, heritage, and culture as a people and keeping it close to them.

We no longer live in rural California, so my children do not understand the farmworker way of life. One thing we do for New Year's is make "Mexican" soup to bring us good luck for the year, and we make tamales during the Christmas season. I've adopted the tradition of having these types of foods as part of our traditional holidays. We now live in the San Francisco Bay Area. We live in a city, but in the rural part of the city, overlooking … you guessed it … vineyards. Maybe my kids do not know the way of life of a farmworker, but my heart is in the peacefulness of the earth and I hope that they learn to respect that as well.

All in all, no matter where I go or where I end up, in my heart and soul, I will always recognize the day-to-day struggle of those who have to "survive." I have fought to survive and hope that I have done so with compassion, love, and hope. I still feel invisible sometimes, and still feel overwhelmed but when I look at the view I know that I am not invisible to God, rather, that he is patiently waiting for my invitation to have coffee with him and invite him into my new home.

Dolores Huerta
National Women's Hall of Fame
Achievement in Humanities

Dolores Huerta is one of the century's most powerful and respected labor movement leaders. Huerta left teaching and cofounded the United Farm Workers with Cesar Chavez in 1962. After teaching grammar school, Dolores left her job because in her words, "I couldn't stand seeing kids come to class hungry and needing shoes. I thought I could do more by organizing farmworkers than by trying to teach their hungry children." Dolores Huerta is the cofounder and Secretary-Treasurer of the United Farm Workers of America, AFL-CIO ("UFW"). The mother of eleven children, fourteen grandchildren, and four great-grandchildren, Dolores has played a major role in the American civil rights movement.

Dolores Huerta, Biography. Accessed December 22, 2010.
http://www.lasculturas.com/aa/bio/bioDoloresHuerta.htm

INTRODUCING SOUL SISTER
KATHLEEN FREIRE-VALDEZ

IT IS INTERESTING TO ME that I chose my cousin Kathleen to be the last of the soul sisters to be introduced in our book *Soul Sisters, Come on to My House*. In many ways, it completes the circle of my life and all the very special women whom I have decided to keep for a lifetime. Kathleen and I share the same name. It is her first name and my middle name. Kathleen and I have known each other from the time we were babies sitting in a high chair and possibly earlier than that.

Kathleen represents to me the Latina part of my family. It was being with Kathleen and at our grandparents' home that we have wonderful memories of a Latino lifestyle and family unit.

I have not written much about my real father, so I will explain now our relationship. My real father did not ever live with me. However, he came and went throughout my life so we never lost contact with him. He financially supported my sister and me until we were out of the home. I never told my real father about the abuse that was going on in my house as a child for fear I would get it more if my stepfather found out about it. My real father did have a heated temper, and I am sure it would have caused much upset if he knew about the abuse. My father always introduced my sister and me with The utmost respect. He would always say, "And these are my beautiful daughters." Much of the time, I did not feel beautiful, but knowing my real father felt that way was all that mattered to me. I was the "apple of his eye," and he would teach me many songs and sing with me the times we shared together. My favorite song was, "You Are My Sunshine," and my father sang that song to me. I owned the moon and the stars when I was with my father and he was not drinking.

The other side was that my father was an alcoholic, and many times he came to visit me as a little girl when he was drinking. This was very upsetting to me, and I now look back and wonder why my mother allowed him to visit with me when he was drunk. As time passed and we all grew up, my father discontinued his drunken behavior around me. Most of all, I will never forget the times I was with my father when I was made to feel so special.

Kathleen is my cousin because our fathers were brothers. They were very close. They loved each other, and they wanted us to love each other and to be close with each other to the end of our days. However, there was much between our lives that took us apart for years, but I can still recall the early days of my childhood and playing with Kathleen at the Christmas season at our grandparents' house. I would have been about five years old and lying on my tummy in my Christmas dress looking at all the beautiful colorful lights on the tree. They were the glass candle lights with the bubbles of colorful liquid going up and down the tube. I was spellbound looking at them. Kathleen was four years old and right next to me with a big smile on her face as we both enjoyed our grandparents' Christmas tree and the family festivities.

As a little girl, Kathleen had a generous and loving heart. It was proven to me the day she gave me her big picture book of Uncle Remus. Boy, did I love that book! I could not believe she actually gave it to me. When we were in our preteens, I went to visit Kathleen at her home off Broadway Street in San Francisco. We played ball in her little backyard, and we had tea at her dining room table with her mother, my Aunt Inga. Kathleen at the time seemed quiet and I did not know why, but I later discovered she was going through a very trying time getting adjusted to her new life and newfound mother.

That summer when I was about twelve, we all went to Disneyland and Santa Monica for two weeks on vacation. I was so glad my uncle and aunt thought to take me with them as company for Kathleen. I loved going with them and having a real vacation; it was something we did not experience much at my home. For two weeks, we picnicked, swam in hotel pools, and went to the beach. I loved Disneyland and could not believe all the fun I was having. One day there, we ran out of bread and were planning a picnic lunch; we had tuna fish on tortillas. I thought it was real funny. Kathleen and I got the giggles in the backseat of the car, and it started to bother her mom. The more my aunt corrected us, the more we would laugh. Yeah, it was great fun to share those innocent times with my cousin Kathleen.

As we grew up and went our separate ways, we never really lost touch with each other. Every other year, there were family reunions, and we would connect there or with our aunts and uncles about each other. As time passed, our parents aged and became ill. After our parents died, Kathleen and I began an even closer relationship.

In February 2009, Kathleen was one of the first persons at our side to care for us when my husband and I returned home from a rehab center after our horrible car accident. My husband had sustained a crushed chest, with heart and lung damage, and multiple leg injuries. He was on oxygen 24-7, and a hospital bed was placed for him in our living room. I had broken my left arm in over twelve places and had seven pins and a rod placed in my upper arm. I decided to stay in the guest bedroom downstairs to be near my husband if he should need me. We were home only one day and had spent only one night at home when Kathleen offered her services to care for us until my brother Anthony could come over for several days. As she drove down my long driveway to reach my home, she discovered a fire engine and response team at our house. My husband had had an anxiety attack at home, and he needed more oxygen. Being completely confused and worried about what was happening, I called 911, and they responded to take him to the hospital.

After driving three hours to reach our house from Santa Rosa, Kathleen immediately offered to take me to the hospital to find my husband. We went to the wrong hospital miles away, only to discover he was in the nearby town of Auburn, six miles from where we lived in Cool, California. After many hours of observation, they released my husband home again, and Kathleen continued to nurse us for several days. I cannot express our gratitude for her kind actions; we were so comforted to know someone else was at our house that cared about us.

Kathleen has been the sister I never really had in life. I have very few positive memories of my own sister. My own sister was mentally ill and chose not to see me even when she herself was dying of breast cancer in July 2009. I honored her last wishes and grieved that we had missed out so much on life by not being close. Kathleen has brought fun, love, laughter, and a warm, loving heart to me. I cherish our relationship and treasure what she and I share. I know in my heart and head that Kathleen will be with me to the very end. It is very comforting to know this because so much in life is uncertain, and it is for this reason she is my soul sister.

Here is her story, and I believe it is a very interesting one.

"La Gata Negra" (The Black Cat)
by Kathleen Freire-Valdez

ON NOVEMBER 11, 1947, MY mother Inga gave birth to a little "love baby" that was me. My parents were madly in love and decided to keep me in hopes that we would someday all be together as a family. I believe that both of my parents were truly in love with each other and also loved me. Unfortunately, my dad had a family and was involved in an unhappy marriage; my mother, although "free," was raised by a very strict German Catholic family. Her life was somewhat limited, although she was a very intelligent, successful young woman. She would have to face and deal with the fact that even though her family was very active in the Catholic church, unfortunately they were bigoted against my dad and his lovely brown skin and his Spanish-speaking family. My birth was a very exciting and fearful time for both of them, and their decision to "keep me" was very loving and admirable.

Upon my mother's recovery, she had the burden of informing her family of my birth. Somehow, she had managed to keep the fact that she was pregnant hidden from her family and now was her time to "step up to the plate," so to speak. As Dad's family was more forgiving and accepting, he had the responsibility of taking care of me. He brought me home to his parents in San Francisco. When my grandmother saw me, she took me in her arms and called me *La Gata Negra*, the black cat! We lived with my grandparents for a short time, and eventually Dad approached his wife with me in his arms and asked if she could help. The timing couldn't have been better, as she had just miscarried a baby girl. I will be forever grateful for her strength and love. I consider myself most fortunate to have had her for "my mommy" and will always lovingly remember her as such.

My first memories of being were on Salinas Avenue in San Francisco. I belonged to my mommy, my dad, my two sisters, and my brother. I remember living in a big house on a hill, with a glass-enclosed sunporch at the top of the front stairs. I shared a bedroom with my brother and our dog named Tippy, who would come in and out during the night. My mommy and daddy slept in the next room, which was huge to me, and my two big sisters slept in a room behind the kitchen near the back door.

I remember my dad leaving for work every morning. I would sit on the toilet seat and watch him shave. He would laugh and talk to me, his eyes always twinkling. We would share a glass of apricot nectar. Then he would take me up in his big strong arms and dance with me in the front room each morning before he left. Before Mommy woke up, I would kneel on the couch for what seemed like hours and sing to him to come back. He was a tall, handsome, Latino man of Ecuadorian and Mexican heritage. He was the first generation on both sides of the family to be born in America. He was bilingual and spoke beautifully in both English and Spanish, although he spoke mostly English to me. Mommy was of Mexican descent. She also was the first of her generation to be born in America. It was from her that I learned my first Spanish words—*agua, montequilla, leche, pan, dulces, pen-pen*, and so on. She would speak to me in Spanish at the table asking, *"Que quieres? Agua, montequilla, leche, pan?"* She would point to each item as she questioned me. She also lapsed into Spanish (which I never understood) when she chased me for coloring the white grout in the bathroom pretty colors with my crayons or painting my lips with her bright red lipstick and wiping it on my new dress or things like that. Because of the hardwood floors, I could never escape. You could hear everything, which later also proved to be good for practicing tap-dance routines.

I loved the house on Salinas Avenue. There were plenty of hiding places for a small child. Lots of cupboards in the kitchen where I could hide, sneak, and listen to my sisters saying and doing things they weren't supposed to. There was a back porch with a small window way up high, just big enough to lean out of and hang clothes from a clothesline or stand on a chair and smell the smells, watch the birds, and look at my grandma's house across the vacant lot. There was a big backyard with a gazebo, which was a great place to have "dirt tea" with my next-door neighbor or to catch a ride on the back of my brother's tricycle on the concrete pathway.

My sense of self, of belonging, of family all stemmed from these early memories, even though I was different—I had red hair. How I longed to have beautiful black hair like my sisters and brother. I could not understand why everybody made such a big thing about my hair color. My understanding was that I would grow up to be like my sisters and my hair would turn black and long.

What I knew to be mine was my Latino family and my daddy, who was absent a lot of the time. He went to work but also did a lot of other things that I didn't understand. Sometimes he would not come home at night, and my mommy would cry. Other times, he would come in late, and Mommy would be upset. Sometimes on the weekends, my Uncle Norbert would come over, and he and my dad would sit at the table and drink whiskey out of little glasses that looked like tiny root-beer mugs and Mommy would ask my *tio* to leave. Of course, no one paid any attention, and the two brothers would carry on for the afternoon. Sometimes he would bring his youngest daughter,

Susan. My older sister, Jean, remembers feeding the two of us in high chairs. We were raised to be very close to each other, just as our dads were.

On special occasions, holidays, or just because, my grandpa—we called him "Papa"—and grandma—we called her "Mama"—would have big family gatherings. The food was Latin, of course, and I remember the good smells of the tortillas frying, the chorizo cooking, and the refried beans warming up. These were happy, festive occasions as all of the family members attended; as the afternoon wore on, everyone danced to mariachi music. All of the cousins would run up and down the stairs, explore the big, dark basement, which was used for winemaking, and play on the porch, hiding under Mama's sewing machine. Family was of the utmost importance to me and made me the happiest of little girls.

The Freire brothers, my dad and my uncle, were very handsome, charming, flirtatious, good mannered, and great dancers; they gained the reputation of "Latin lovers" quite early in life. I believe that this was a kind of macho belief that was handed down to them. It had quite a big influence on their personal self-image and their seemingly all-embracing love of life, family, women, and song. This was to become an even bigger influence on my life beginning at the age of five.

When I turned five years old, life as I knew it suddenly changed. My daddy took me away to live with him and my real mother. As my birth mother had come to visit me at times during the year, I knew who she was, but I could not grasp the fact that she was my mother. It took some time to realize and embrace the fact that I had two mothers, both of them unique and different as night and day. My birth mother was German and Norwegian. My mommy was Mexican. My birth mother was an executive secretary. My mommy was a stay-at-home mom. My birth mother was tall and blonde. My mommy was short and shapely. Suddenly it seemed that my whole world had changed. Where was my familiar Latin family?

I was enrolled in Catholic school and had to wear a uniform. The nuns were strange to me, and I distinctly remember the smell of the highly polished marble floors when you entered the building. It was strange and made me nauseous. I did not know any of the other kids, and I had to go to a place they called a "dayhome" after school because my mother worked. It was all so strange and confusing.

I was sick most of the first year of my new life. My dad was everything to me. He would take me to visit Mommy on Salinas Avenue but had to stop as it was too painful for both of us to part again.

To this day, my older sis tells me how much they all missed me. I remember getting very excited when we could talk on the phone. Thank God that we visited my grandparents and cousins frequently. I missed everyone so much.

My sisters would reenter my life when I was a preteen. Mommy and I kept in touch through cards, letters, and my cousin Ana, who would come to visit her dad, Herman Farrell, who was Dad's best friend; she would take messages back to Mommy, who was now living in Sunnyvale. The next time I saw Mommy was when I was fourteen. My very first boyfriend drove me to her home in Sunnyvale, and we spent the day together. We were both so happy. From then on, I made it a point to keep in contact with her. She was the first to know about my pregnancy, and she gave me the phone number of our old family doctor so I could confirm the pregnancy. She threw me a shower at her home in Sunnyvale, and she held my daughter shortly after her birth. She was in my life until February 1, 2010, when she passed away at age ninety-four. I will always be grateful for her love and will continue to hold her in my heart. She gave me so much of the love and strength that I feel today.

We now lived in a garden apartment only one block from the school. Upon entering, you could see right into my mother's bedroom, and she had the most beautiful vanity I had ever seen. It had a large round mirror and was made out of the prettiest wood; it even had a little cushioned seat that you tucked under it when you stood up and left the room. It had a pretty good-size kitchen, and the front room overlooked the garden. A neighbor's cat named Cookie would come in for a visit on the weekends. I eventually adapted, though it took about a year or so, and made friends and grew to love my mother, school, and everyday environment. New things were expected of me, and I was able to conform and meet my new standards. I went from a Latino household to a white household. Luckily, I was able to enjoy both environments. Dad was beginning his successful climb of both the corporate and social ladder, and my mother was a successful executive secretary. I managed to achieve a B average and enjoy my new friends and school. My summers and holidays were spent with many "second" mothers, so to speak.

Marie and Herman Farrell, who were very close friends of my parents, stepped in. Tio Herman, who was a construction worker, would pick me up from school, and I spent the afternoons with them in their big Victorian house on Steiner Street in San Francisco, which I loved. Summertime would find me there for a while. I was with Marie the summer of her pregnancy. We would go out to her backyard, rub baby oil on ourselves, and sit in the sun until we were nice and brown. She was a beautiful Mexican woman from a humble background. Her father was a migrant worker. I don't know the family history, but he must have done very well to be able to buy one of the "Old Lady Victorians" on Steiner Street. From her, I learned contentment and happiness. She was always happy and smiling; she made you feel so special when you came to visit her. My own daughter shares the same feeling and experience. Marie especially loved all of the children of her family, extended family, and friends.

I also spent time with my Tia Emma in Daly City and the San Bruno area. She would invite me in for cream of wheat in the morning, and we would watch TV and eat breakfast together. My cousin, Julio, would be home sometimes, and we would play together outside. Tia Emma was always so happy, as she is still to this day. Her younger sister Gabriella says that Tia Emma has the ability to make herself happy at anytime. I remember laughing a lot with her and still do. She is ninety-four and still spunky. She is learning how to play pool and play the harmonica, and she was taking pottery classes. Tia Emma taught me happiness = enjoyment of life and who you are.

My grandparents also invited me into their home. My grandpa was a beautiful gardener. He seemed to know so many things and was always patient with me, showing me many of his ways. His backyard was transformed into an enchanting garden. When my grandfather built the house in San Francisco, the backyard was used for raising chickens, rabbits, and goats. The three Freire brothers were assigned to tending each of the animals: Lucian (Luciano) *conejos* (rabbits), Alejandro (Alexander) *lechivas* (goats), and Norberto, the *gallinas (chickens).* But, because he was the baby and not as big in size as his brothers, he did not have to tend the chickens and my dad had the extra chore of helping my grandpa with the feeding and butchering for suppers

As there was no need for the livestock when my generation came into the world, Papa did another thing that he loved best, which was gardening. Summers spent in the warm, sunny backyard were filled with fragrant smells, bountiful fruits, and lovely blooms and blossoms of all of God's glory. He built little pathways, walkways, arbors where you could walk through an arbor of passion flowers overhead and trailing down to you. You could walk on little paths lined with brick through many fruit trees—peaches, apricots, pears, and apples. If you looked down, you would find tomatoes, yerba buena, and lettuce. On the other side of the main walkway would be the most beautiful roses you could ever imagine. He joined an exclusive rose club and would buy unusual roses, such as the "purple" rose, and raise them to perfection. The bird of paradise was one of his favorites.

He was also a handyman of sorts. I remember one time when a small heel broke off my shoe, he was able to fix it in minutes. By that time, he had given up on the winemaking. It always still smelled of wine in his basement. One of our favorite things to do as grandchildren was to look at and play with all of the strange things that he would bring back from his sailing. He traveled around the world six times and imported many fine treasures for family members and furniture for his home. I will always remember Papa as a very loving man who put his family first. I loved who he was and what he did. He did get to meet my daughter, and so the beat goes on. From Papa, I learned the joy of family and how it molds your character, all-encompassing love, joy of giving life, nurturing, and passion for the people and things that you love.

My grandma was just as influential in my life. She loved to sing and would listen to Mexican music and sing along with it. She showed me how to dance as she had done when she was a young woman, balancing a tray of glasses on her head and swishing her big skirt around. She loved to sing and whistle to the canaries that Papa would bring back to her from the Orient. She showed me how to make chicken soup with the feet in it. On certain occasions, she would make calamari with the ink sac left in it, and I would love how purple it looked over white rice. When we took the bus downtown, she would ask me how to say certain words in English so she could ask the bus driver herself. Mama taught herself how to speak English by listening to the radio and T.V. Other times, she would see me getting bored and would come downstairs and play ball with me in front of their house on Key Avenue in San Francisco. Mama did not let language become a barrier between us. She took great care to make herself understood and to let me know how much she cared. The first time I brought my daughter Rose to meet her grandparents, Mama held her and told me to cover her little fists with socks so she wouldn't scratch herself. She would stroke her baby nose so it wouldn't get too big.

The very last time I saw her was when she was still living with Tia Emma. She had become very frail, but she still remembered me and we shared a glass of red wine at the table. She told me that she would be joining Papa in heaven soon and that she loved me. Mama showed me unconditional love, strength, perseverance, acceptance, and self-pride. I consider myself most fortunate to have spent so much time with her and to learn her ways. These are the people with whom I grew up. They let me stay with them for as long as I needed to, and to all of them I am very grateful. Tia Emma is still here—we talk on the phone—and all of the others are in my heart. Even though they have passed on, I will never forget them, all that we shared, and all that they taught me.

Upon entering high school, I was trusted to stay by myself after school. I learned how to jump-start dinner for my mother so she wouldn't have so much to do when she came home after work. We now lived in a large San Francisco flat on Broadway and Hyde Streets. My parents would walk to work every day, which was no small task in itself. As they both worked in the financial district, they walked up and down the big hills together. I would walk up three hills to the bus stop. To this day, I think we all were part goat! I loved this flat. It had lots of light and was airy—and I had my very own bedroom. When I turned fourteen, my parents told me I could redo my room. I chose a blue rug and blue paint for the walls. I chose a rosebud-print bedspread with matching pillow shams, white nylon Priscilla curtains, and a big blond dresser with a big mirror and matching nightstands and chest of drawers. (My parents used this set, I have it now, and I will be giving it to my daughter this year.) My mother bought me an oval-shaped perfume tray with a mirror on the bottom surrounded by gold leaves. This was my very first bedroom, and I felt pretty lucky and grown up.

As long as I went to summer school, I was pretty much on my own while my parents worked during the day. After class, I helped out with chores, hanging clothes on the clothesline, ironing, dusting, and so on, and would walk down to the marina to visit my best friend, Julia. When summer school was over, we would walk to Aquatic Park or Fisherman's Wharf, go to a movie, or just hang out. I loved it that she was Italian, as it was very close to Mexican/Ecuadorian.

I enjoyed my teen years, even though my parents were very strict. Phone calls were limited to ten minutes on school nights, and no boys could call until I was sixteen. Sixteen seemed to be the magical age. I was looking forward to being able to shave my legs, wear makeup, have "legal" boyfriends, and be allowed to date. Of course, being a teenager, I was very impatient and did a few things on my own—quite a few things. At age seventeen, I graduated from Presentation High School in San Francisco about three months pregnant.

Having taken business courses in high school, I had already applied for jobs so I could go right to work. Unfortunately, I did not realize at that time that I could not be pregnant and work. My parents were heartbroken. My dad cried, and my mother was very angry with me. They had envisioned a very different life for me, one not filled with the hardships that they had had to go through. Nevertheless, my mother went ahead and planned the wedding. My parents drove us up to Reno on the July Fourth weekend. I was married in my graduation suit (which was by now too tight), and we spent the evening in a motel in separate rooms—I and my husband, Sam, in one room, and my mother and dad in another room. I felt very strange. On the drive back, my mother went over reception plans with me and the invitation list. They threw us a fun reception in my grandparents' backyard in the new patio house that my Tio Pop had built for them. We managed to have fun and smashed cake in each other's faces. I still get in trouble for it! To this day, I'm sorry for disappointing them and can fully understand and appreciate their love and good intentions. Once again, I was given the gift of unconditional love as it paved the way for my life journey.

My daughter, Rose, was born on December 20, 1965, weighing in at 6.7 pounds and twenty-one inches long. She was tiny and all red and so cute. I dressed her in red and put her under the Christmas tree for her daddy's Christmas present. Being a young mother was a joy, a challenge, and very lonely. My parents continued to support us but kept a distance now. They also needed time to adjust to their relationship. My mother-in-law, Dolores, helped me a great deal as she was not working. Although Dolores and I are no longer as close as we were, she has been and is still a big part of my daughter's life as well as her father Sam. Our young marriage (him at age nineteen and me at seventeen) lasted approximately ten years. I started working part-time at an office job when Rose was three and a half, and by the time she was ten, I was permanent part-time at Macy's San Francisco. Our young family started out in a Dolger apartment in Westlake, moved to Hayes and Masonic during the hippie days, and ended up in the Sunset on Seventh Avenue. This was the last home we would ever live in together as a family. Our marriage ended and I took an apartment just four blocks away so Rose could ride her bike down and spend the night. I was pretty wild in those days. I felt energy, excitement, and the need for exploration. I also saw myself as a kind of "folksy, hippie, model" type. Drugs came into my life, as they were in just about everyone's in our age group. What harm could they do? Timothy Leary did LSD!

The major regret that I have about drugs is not being more aware of the effect they could possibly have on my daughter. We all learn a great deal by example. I feel I could have been a better teacher in this respect. About twelve years later, I learned a big life lesson. Addiction rears its ugly head in so many different people and places. Today, I give thanks daily for Rose's strength to overcome her fear, face her dependence, move on, become happy, and bring great joy to her family. She is a most fantastic human being! We all love her and cherish her. Once again, unconditional love!

My second marriage took place in San Francisco City Hall. Rose was about thirteen and was my maid of honor! She looked very pretty. She did not know what to make of it and later decided that she didn't want to have anything to do with the idea of a stepfather. I do not blame her, and neither does he (Pete). She was already going through a difficult time (being thirteen), and this was just icing on the cake for her. We all survived.

In between times (about 1978), my mother had a major stroke. She was working for the Bank of California in San Francisco, and I was working at SF Macy's. We would sometimes meet for lunch or for cocktails after work. One of her fellow employees called me from the bank and informed me that my mother was taken to Seton Medical Center in Daly City after she had collapsed at work. Just as I received the phone call, Pete walked up to my counter. What a blessing! He drove me to the hospital right away. I was not driving as I didn't have a car, and Dad was out of town on business. I remember seeing my mother for the first time in the hospital in ICU. She was hooked up to tubes, looked very distressed, and was crying. She kept apologizing to me, and I remember feeling so sorry for her and holding her as best I could, trying to console her. Marie and Herman Farrell came right after work and stayed with me while we waited for my dad to come. We did not even know if he had gotten the message, and my mother kept asking for him. My dad arrived the next day. By the time he received the message, it was too late for him to drive up that day. My mother was paralyzed on her whole left side. At first she could not speak, walk, or use her left side in any way. The doctor told her that she would never walk again. After months of therapy, one day she walked into the doctor's office and thumbed her nose at him. She was a very determined German! She also went on to give lectures to other stroke victims, and one of her speeches was written up in the newspaper. My daughter is strong just like her grandma!

I carry my mother in my heart and often remember her words. She was a very beautiful, intelligent woman, had a way with words, and instilled a great belief in me that everything would work out in its own time. She had all of the faith in the world that Rose would return to us—she even gave me an age. She told me that by the time Rose turned forty, she would "have her head on straight." After thinking long and hard about this, I came to agree with her, as that was when things started to turn for me also for the better. My mother was wise, loving, intelligent, strong, and always a lady. She never really said anything bad about anyone and always kept a positive attitude. Even though she was given a hard path to follow after being stricken by a major stroke, she hung in there, did the best she could, proved her doctors wrong, and was the best partner/wife my dad could ever have. Their relationship was touching. He stayed with her and was her caregiver for a good twenty-five years after her stroke, and she remained by his side, always wanting the best for him. Their relationship is another story in itself.

Unfortunately, my second marriage did not last very long—about four years. We both agreed that we got along much better when we weren't married and we should have maybe kept it like that. We parted on mostly pleasant terms.

Life found me in my thirties then. Still working at Macy's and living in the Sunset on Twenty-First Avenue. Rose was getting older and wanting her freedom and privacy. We did share one thing that was quite surprising. We loved to crank up the music and clean house together on Saturdays. We enjoyed the flat on Twenty-First Avenue for only a couple more years. The owner wanted to sell the building and was kicking out his two tenants. My parents came over while I was packing, helped me with a small load, and came to see my new apartment on Eighteenth Avenue in the Castro. Dad brought his toolbox and put up pictures and fixed the venetian blinds for me. They also gave me a check to help me out. They were always there for me, even when I screwed up. I still feel them. I hope I can always do the same for my daughter.

When I was about thirty-four, I was working for a drugstore chain and helping them set up a new store at Levi's Plaza along the Embarcadero. As this was a brand-new plaza, all of the buildings were either new or under construction. Our drugstore had barely been finished when we moved in and started getting shipments of items to set up in the new store. It was very exciting as I was being transferred from the original store in Embarcadero #2. At the same time, right across the plaza, a new restaurant was being built. It was sometime in January 1982. I can remember the harsh rain and was surprised that the construction workers were still working. They were a friendly bunch and would come in the store on their breaks and buy candy, sodas, and after work, a six-pack of beer. They would always make us laugh when they came in and flirted with us and joked around. One of these men was to become my third husband. His name was Thomas C. Valdez.

At first, Tom was very shy. I had already talked to his friend Doug, who was more outgoing, so Tom would come over with Doug to be formally introduced. He started coming over once a day, then twice, then three times, and so on. Finally in March, he got up the nerve to ask me out. I refused, saying my mother had had a stroke and I had to go and tend to her. This went on for another month until I couldn't use this excuse anymore, and he finally asked me for my phone number. I gave him my work number, feeling that it would limit the conversation time.

He was very persistent. When he came to my counter with his coveralls on and his hard hat in his hands and asked me out to dinner and a comedy club that Saturday evening, I agreed. Our first date took place on May 22, 1982. He surprised me when he came to pick me up. I opened the door, and he was holding a bouquet of a dozen red roses interspersed with baby's breath and a card that said, "You knock my lights out!" I found him surprisingly fun to be around and easy to talk to. He had a kind of calm and quiet about him and was willing to listen. His green Oldsmobile Cutlass was immaculate, and you could tell that he was very proud of it. He drove with ease, and I felt very safe with him. He listened to salsa music and played it for me, telling me the history of the musicians and the music. It felt good to be in touch with my Latin roots again. He brought back memories of my family background. He spoke very enunciated English, was very clean, smelled nice, and seemed to be pretty well educated. He was tall, dark, and handsome, with a full mustache and beautiful, expressive, large brown eyes. I liked the way he gently touched my shoulder or waist, not being overbearing at all. I was quite impressed with him that evening.

After our first date, he continued to come into the store and make me laugh. We started going to lunch together, and then to a movie on the weekend. Soon we were dating more frequently and started to see each other every weekend. As he lived in a rather large apartment in Alameda, I would take the bus to his apartment after work on Friday, or if he was working in the city, he would wait around until five o'clock and pick me up from work. My daughter was almost eighteen at this time and preferred to have her weekends with her friends as much as possible. We stayed in touch by phone, and for the most part, things worked out okay.

One important fact that I have left out is that Tom, from day 1—our first date—told me that he couldn't drink. He was an alcoholic. I had never considered anything like this before, so being very naïve, I urged him to have just one cocktail with me. Unfortunately, he gave in, and thus the spiral started. We were to share twenty-eight years of our lives together, almost half of which were drinking and half of which were sober (for him). In the early part of our relationship, the drinking gradually progressed. I, being the "party girl," didn't think much of it. In fact, I joined him in morning drinks before work for a couple of weeks. Thank God, my body couldn't take it, so I stopped. He was unable to stop, and it went from bad to worse.

By 1989, seven years from when we first dated, Tom was pretty sick. I had invited him to move in with me in my one-bedroom apartment on Guerrero Street. Work was slow for him that year, and he was having trouble keeping up with his rent and bills. When we first started dating, he was very generous helping me out to pay my rent and bills. I wanted to return the favor if I could. I thought that I could "cure him," and I also loved him and wanted him to be permanently in my life. He wasn't working, was very sick, and took to roaming the streets during the day when I was at work. I got in contact with a close union friend of his, Edward, and begged for help. I was afraid that Tom would die. Edward took Tom into his home in San Leandro and convinced him to enroll in a twenty-eight-day sobriety, live-in program. Fortunately for Tom, the union, Local 518, that he belonged to sponsored it through a program called "Beat It." He lived for twenty-eight days at Maynord's Recovery Center in Sonora. He wrote me quite frequently, and his letters and cards gave me hope.

When Tom returned to me in late May, he was a changed person. His first weekend home, we went to the Carnival parade on Mission Street. Everyone was walking the streets with some kind of alcoholic beverage in a paper bag. Tom did not even give it a second thought. I could hardly believe my eyes and ears. Tom was a totally changed, gentle, quiet, peaceful man who seemed to be as much in love with me as I was with him. He opened up and told me about his experience at Maynord's and how grateful he was to be given the chance to recover. He sought out the nearest AA meeting place and became secretary to the group; he would go in early to make the coffee. He knew all of the meeting schedules, went to several meetings in one day, and was very diligent about reading the Big Book. He would speak to me about meetings and how he felt they were important to him; he would quote to me out of the Big Book if he felt one of our egos was inflated. He had a sincere appreciation of life now, and his life began to turn around, as did mine.

We found ourselves moving to a two-bedroom apartment in Millbrae. I had found a good job in the very southern end of San Francisco, right by Candlestick, for a concrete subcontractor. Work had picked up for Tom, and he was working full-time and even some overtime. He continued to go to meetings even in Millbrae and would sometimes still make the trip to the city to attend those meetings as well. We were happy. He took me to San Antonio, Texas, to meet his dad and all of his friends. We made it part of our yearly vacation to visit his dad. The other part was the yearly reunion at Maynord's in Sonora. I loved going to Sonora. We had a favorite place to stay, California Inns of Sonora. There was an outdoor swimming pool and hot tub. The weather was hot way after nine o'clock in the evening, and we would swim outdoors and stargaze. Mornings would find us in the hot tub relaxing with our coffee.

The weekend days, Saturday and Sunday, we were at Maynord's. They were days of meetings, bingo, volleyball, and barbeque. Sometimes they would have a sober rock band. Each year, Tom would go up to the podium to receive his sobriety birthday chip and always say a little something, making sure to always thank me in front of the whole group. He was able to collect fifteen chips. We always ended the day holding hands in a big circle, reciting the serenity prayer and ending with, *"Keep coming back!"* I really enjoyed this special weekend. I enjoyed seeing Tom so involved and watching him realize how much he needed to keep participating and how much they had helped him and me. I enjoyed the people, as they seemed so sincere and always ready to share thoughts and hugs. The whole circle experience was so joyful for me that it often brought me to tears. I just loved the fact that a group of strangers could come together and share one cause and put it in God's hands.

Our relationship continued to grow in a positive way. We were becoming very stable in our jobs. Once we had relocated to Millbrae, Tom was accepted by my parents and all of the family, and they all seemed to get along well. My dad was especially good to him and often bragged about him to his golf buddies; he tried to make Tom feel like he was loved and appreciated. We lived in the Millbrae area for approximately ten years. We finally got married in 1997 and always joked about having the longest engagement in history—fifteen years.

My parents had relocated to Rohnert Park in 1986. As they grew older, we began to spend more time with them. Every other weekend, we would drive up to meet them for brunch and spend the day or the entire weekend with them. In 1998, the housing boom was in full bloom. One weekend, on my way back to Millbrae, I stopped in Petaluma to see some of the new housing developments. I liked what I saw and talked Tom into coming up the next weekend to check it out with me. We especially liked one new housing tract on the east side. We waited a few months before going back, and by that time there were only two homes left. We settled on the corner home, signed some papers, and before we knew it, we moved to Petaluma in November just in time for my fiftieth birthday! Once again, my parents stepped in to help us out. They were so excited that we were moving closer to them they couldn't do enough for us. They treated us to the extras, like the air-conditioner and the venetian blinds. They were even waiting for us with pizza and beer when our four trucks full of friends and furniture arrived on moving day. Dad took pictures of our house in each phase of the building. We were all very happy and excited.

Life in Petaluma was quite a bit different than Millbrae. It seemed to be more country-style living to us. Weekends would find us driving down to the city or to Millbrae for a while. We finally adapted and came to appreciate and love the many things that Sonoma County had to offer. We still kept our jobs in San Francisco. All too soon we learned about "the commute." We each spent at least four hours on the road each day and on some days five to six hours. I finally gave up my job in San Francisco and decided to try my luck at job hunting up here. After a few trials and errors, I finally found an electrical subcontractor who needed someone like me to manage the office for him. The job was only five minutes away from my parents' home. They were thrilled, and of course, I would have lunch at their house every day and stop by for a glass of wine on my way home from work. Tom continued to commute back and forth to the city. He had retired from the glaziers' union and went to work for the city and county of San Francisco Glazing Department. His plan was to stay for five years and become vested, so we both would have medical and dental benefits for life. He was successful in carrying it out, and I am completely grateful to him for that. As he said, "It was an act of love" —and it was.

I worked for the electrical subcontractor for seven years. In November 2003, I went to lunch at my parents' home as usual. Dad answered the door and said that my mother had had a bad night and was not feeling well. I kissed her hello and noticed that she looked pale and very frail. I asked her if she was all right, and she complained of a pain in her neck on the right side and asked me to look and see if it was bruised. Nothing was noticeable, so I offered to get her an aspirin to ease the pain. I brought it back to her; she took it and assured me that she would be okay, so I went to the kitchen to serve her soup and get my lunch. Dad was seated at the table. I heard my mother utter a strange, muffled noise, and I asked Dad if she was okay. He didn't hear me, as he was very hard of hearing, so I went in to see for myself. Mother was slumped over in her wheelchair, and Dad didn't even know it. I shouted for him to help me with the chair, immediately dialed 911, and proceeded to give her mouth-to-mouth resuscitation. She passed away very quickly from a massive stroke. Both Dad and I were very grateful that I was there. Her death changed all of our lives. Once again, I carry her in my heart.

Dad was brokenhearted. He hated being alone and not having her to care for. Tom and I took care of all of her belongings, as it made him cry to look at them. Dad was very sentimental. He ran from their home and spent most of his time in Walnut Creek with another widow in the family and her sisters. This made him happy, so for that I was grateful. The following year, Dad had a bad gallbladder and drove himself up from Walnut Creek. We checked him into Kaiser, and he had it removed. God works in mysterious ways. Nothing like this had happened to him when he was caretaking my mother.

In 2004, Dad was diagnosed with pancreatic cancer. He survived the operation and returned to spend a few nights with me in Petaluma. Most of his recovery took place at his home in Rohnert Park. He was living alone, so I became his caregiver. For three years, he lived cancer free. All the family enjoyed being with him, and everyone would gather together as much as possible. He was a great dad, the first love of our lives, and we were all "Daddy's" girls. He was so sweet and loving and made each and every one of us feel special. In 2007, the cancer returned. He lost his battle with cancer and passed on July 22. I was with him until the end. I will never forget him and will carry him in my heart always.

Through all of this living and dying, Tom was going through some major changes himself. He hated his commute and could not get beyond it. He became cranky and irritable. Work was turning sour on him. The guys he worked with were very cliquey and would team up on him, tease him, and play mean jokes on him. They liked to party after work and would make fun of Tom because he was in AA. Unfortunately, the commute, the criticism, and the ridiculing were too much for him to bear, and he surrendered to his addiction and started drinking again. This was the beginning of his demise. Life began a downward spiral for us. The more he drank, the more we fought. He was upset with me for spending more time with Dad than with him. I tried to shine him on. I was holding down a forty-hour-a-week job, taking care of Dad, which included cooking extra at dinner so Dad could have dinner for the next evening to heat up in the microwave, trying to get a half-hour walk in each night for myself, cooking dinner, and trying to spend some time with Tom. It wasn't working. He was becoming more resentful toward me, Dad, and then the whole family.

Tom retired from the city in 2007. I moved in with Dad in May of that year just in time to take him to the hospital. I stayed at Dad's house for about a year until I sold it. During that time, Tom would call me every day and evening, come to have lunch, and spend the afternoon with me. I sold Dad's home and moved into a condo in Santa Rosa. Our relationship remained the same, except that we began to see more of each other. In 2009, I realized that Tom was sick. I moved back into our Petaluma house to be with him and take care of him. For the first half of 2009, he could tolerate his stomach and shoulder pain. In August, he started to be sick to his stomach and have diarrhea as much as three times a week. In September, he was not looking so good and was getting sick more frequently. The last trip that we took together was to visit cousin Susan in Cool. Tom insisted on driving both ways, up and back. That was his last road trip.

On September 29, I rushed him to the emergency room with internal bleeding. He had been bleeding all night and didn't want to tell me, but he finally did. The emergency staff did a wonderful job and saved his life. He had literally been bleeding to death.I found out what he had known all along: he had cirrhosis of the liver and partial renal failure. We began the fight for his life. He would be eligible for a new liver in February 2010. He was very committed to getting well and fought long and hard. I was very proud of him for his perseverance and stamina. Even though this was the most horrible experience I had ever had, I wanted to be there with him; it brought us closer together, and we were at last able to express our eternal love for each other. I stayed overnight with him in the hospital. The nurse woke me up when it was his time, and I said, "Good-bye," and watched him take his last breath.

He passed peacefully without pain on January 5, 2010, just nine days before his birthday. He would have been fifty-nine. Once again, he lives on in my heart. I am grateful for all of the good years that we shared and the wonderful life we had—good times and bad. He had a heart of gold and was truly a very sensitive, intelligent, and loving man. He made sure that I would live on in comfort and not have to worry. As he told me in his last hours, "I love you with all of my heart and soul" —as I do you, my Tom.

The year 2010 had a very rough beginning for me, having lost two of the closest people in my life. Although I am still grieving, I can reflect and learn from my parents once again. Just as they had taught me about life, they also taught me about death. They taught me how much a part of life death is and that even though one has to let go of our loved ones on earth, they will remain with us in spirit. Just as I recovered from each of their deaths, so now will I recover from my most recent losses.

Gracious a Dios para todos ellos! Los amare para siempre!
Thanks be to God for all of them! I will love them forever!

"The greatest degree of inner tranquility comes from the development of love and compassion. The more we care for the happiness of others, the greater is our own sense of well-being."
—Tenzin Gyatso, the fourteenth Dalai Lama

10 Inspiring Quotes for a Depressed Heart. Accessed December 22, 2010. http://www.beliefnet.com/Health/Emotional-Health/Depression/

CONCLUSION

It's December 20, 2010, just five days before Christmas, and I've just completed the writing of *Soul Sisters, Come on to My House*. I've learned a lot in the past couple of years, more than I thought I would learn. I've learned so much more from my soul sisters about their lives, dreams, and desires. They are such wonderful women. I have learned that you never really know anyone, but the more you listen with compassion, the more you learn to understand ... our life experiences are what make all of us who we are today.

We all have choices to make, such as improving relationships with others we know little about. In turn, we learn to extend our own knowledge of others' lives and cultures. I can clearly say now that if you do not open your mind and heart to someone, you will be missing out on one of life's greatest joys. Oprah Winfrey said it so clearly: "Did you hear me? Did you hear what I had to say? And did what I say matter?"

After five surgeries in less than two years, I have learned a lot about myself as well. My husband's injuries have all healed. He has lost a considerable amount of strength since the accident and the healing process. I continue to go to physical therapy and do many exercises every day to build up my own strength in my arms. We have defined a new normal for us now, and I hope to improve more in strength over time.

However, all is not lost because we have continued our love of travel. When I was in Avignon, France, in May 2010, I visited *le Palais des Papes* (the Pope's Palace). Right next to it is a beautiful cathedral called Our Lady of Doms. One of my passions is to visit cathedrals and churches, whether they are in small country villages or grand cities. As I entered the cathedral, I visited a special area where there was a statue of the Virgin Mary holding the baby Jesus. I was deep in prayer when my husband was taking photos. He caught my attention and said, "Susan, this is really interesting. I tried three times to take a picture of you, and there is this light coming through the stained-glass window over the Madonna and onto your shoulders. When I click the camera, it does not pick up the beam of light." Well, now he really had my attention, and I asked him to stand where I was standing, and I looked through the camera. He was right—the light is not picked up by the camera. I smiled at him and said, "Well, I guess I'm blessed." I thought to myself: *Another miracle has happened to me on this vacation.*

At home, I collect rosary beads from all of my travels, and I keep them in my prayer room. My cousin Kathleen had sent me a special pair, and they had writing on the back of some of the beads. We discovered it is the Prayer of St. Francis. It asks for strength to give of ourselves to meet the needs of others. As I read the message on the beads, I realized this is the essence of peace within.

It reads:

> Where there is hatred, sow love;
> Where there is injury, pardon;
> Where there is doubt, faith;
> Where there is despair, hope;
> Where there is darkness, light;
> Where there is sadness, joy.

While on the Internet, I found the rest of the prayer, which states, "Grant that I may not so much seek to be consoled as to console; to be understood as to understand; to be loved as to love. For it is in giving that we receive; it is in pardoning that we are pardoned; and it is in dying that we are born to eternal life."

In conclusion, this book was not written to question or judge whether you believe in God or a higher power. It was not written to influence or persuade Christianity or any other religion. The purpose is to educate and inform readers about others' beliefs and values. Religion plays a major role in many people's lives. It determines how we think, how we process information, and how we live our lives on a daily basis. Religion and spirituality are important elements when writing about the human spirit and how it may impact cultural sensitivity.

When we think about it, how easy and how simple it is to care about others, and receiving the gift of giving makes a better world for all. I hope you enjoyed reading *Soul Sisters, Come on to My House*. I hope it will help you understand the meaning of learning from each other and the wonderful gift of sharing and listening to understand with compassion. Human kindness and how we treat each other will define who we are as a person.

After three years, I'm glad I waited for the time needed to write this book; by waiting and taking pauses, I learned so much more in the process. For example, *Soul Sisters, Come on to My House* evolved into what it was meant to do ... to deliver the true message of human kindness.

In the end, I'm glad my soul sisters did come to my house. We did it! We accomplished writing a book about cultural diversity and our life experiences. We wanted to share with others that in spite of what we endured, we came to understand the true meaning of life ... human kindness. Love and peace bring happiness within and are to be shared with others.

Be brave. Take the next step in your journey to human kindness. Seek and you shall find your soul sister(s), and maybe you will even find a soul brother or two. Discover how you want to be defined.

One Heart, One Mind

We must stand together, the four sacred colors of humanity, as the one family that we are, in the interest of peace. We must abolish nuclear and conventional weapons of war. We must raise leaders of peace. We must unite the religions of the world as a spiritual force strong enough to prevail in peace. We human beings are a spiritual energy that is a thousand times stronger than nuclear energy. Our energy is the combined will of all people with the spirit of the natural world, to be the one body, one heart, and one mind for peace.

Leon Shenandoah, Tadadaho,
Iroquois Six Nations
November 22, 1993, Cry of the Earth

Steven McFadden, *The Little Book of Native American Wisdom*
(Rockport, MA: Element, 1994), 36.

BIBLIOGRAPHY

Alice Walker. Brainy Quote. Accessed December 22, 2010. http://brainyquote.com/quotes/authors/a/alice_walker/2.html

"Dolores Huerta, Biography." Accessed December 22, 2010. http://www.lasculturas.com/aa/bio/bioDoloresHuerta.htm

Kaiser Permanente National Diversity Council and the Kaiser Permanente National Diversity Department. *A Provider's Handbook on Culturally Competent Care: African American Population,* 2nd Edition. 2003, 3–6.

Kaiser Permanente National Diversity Council. *A Provider's Handbook on Culturally Competent Care: Latino Population.* 1996. 5, 6, 11, and 15.

Leon Shenandoah, Tadadaho, Iroquois Six Nations. Steven McFadden, *The Little Book of Native American Wisdom.*(Rockport, MA: Element Inc., 1994), 36.

Mae Jemison. Jone Lewis Johnson, "About.com Women's History." Accessed December 22, 2010. http://womenshistory.about.com/od/quotes/a/mae_jemison.htm

Mary Eliza Mahoney, Biography. Accessed March 31, 2011. http://www.asu.edu/nursing/sources/nur361/leader13/biography.html

"Quotations by Author," Eleanor Roosevelt Quotes—The Quotations Page. Accessed December 22, 2010. http://www.quotationspage.com/quotes/Eleanor_Roosevelt. 1.

Sojourner Truth. Jack Canfield, Mark Victor Hansen, Lisa Nichols, and Tom Joyner, *Chicken Soup for the African American Soul.*(Deerfield Beach, Florida: Health Communications, Inc. 2004), viii.

Tenzin Gyatso, the fourteenth Dalai Lama. 10 Inspiring Quotes for a

Depressed Heart. Accessed December 22, 2010. http://www.beliefnet.com/Health/Emotional -Health/ Depression/

"The Building Block of Character," Helen Keller. 10 Inspiring Quotes for a Depressed Heart. Accessed December 22, 2010. http://www.beliefnet.com/HealthEmtional-Health Depression/

Personal Cultural Diversity Reading List

Anne Fadiman, *The Spirit Catches You and You Fall Down* (New York: Farrar, Straus, and Giroux, 1997).

Jack Canfield, Mark Victor Hansen, Jennifer Read Hawthorne, and Marci Shimoff, *A Second Chicken Soup for the Women's Soul* (Deerfield Beach, Florida: Health Communications Inc. 1998)

Jack Canfield, Mark Victor Hansen, Lisa Nichols, and Tom Joyner, *Chicken Soup for the African American Soul* (Deerfield Beach, Florida: Health Communications, Inc. 2004)

Joseph Epes Brown, *Animals of the Soul* (Rockport, MA: Element, 1997)

Mariton Barrera, Kevin Mundey, Debbie Schanbacher, Bob Shilling, and Shirley Simmons. *The Little Book of Sign Language* (Philadelphia, Pennsylvania: Running Press 2000)

Michael Powell, *Behave Yourself!* (Bogota, Colombia: The Globe Pequot Press, 2005)

Milton Meltzer, *A History of the American Negro* (New York: Apollo Edition, 1967)

R. David Edmunds, *Studies in Diversity American Indian Leaders* (University of Nebraska Press: Lincoln and London 1980)

R. Roosevelt Thomas, Jr., and Marjorie I. Woodruff, *Building a House for Diversity* (New York: AMA Publications 1999)

T. C. McLuhan, *Touch the Earth* (New York: Simon and Schuster 1971)